# Look out for a
# FREE MASK
## Inside this Annual!

D1505310

## You Will Need:

- Thin elastic, wool or string

- Scissors

- Sticky Tape

## Instructions:

1. Pull out the perforated mask page.
2. Pop out the mask.
3. Cut enough elastic/wool/string to fit around the back of your head.
4. Attach to the back of the mask with some sticky tape.
5. Have fun with your new mask!

**SCISSORS ARE SHARP! ASK AN ADULT FOR HELP BEFORE USING.**

# SHOOT

Published 2013.

Pedigree Books Limited, Beech Hill House, Walnut Gardens, Exeter, Devon EX4 4DH

www.pedigreebooks.com
shoot@pedigreegroup.co.uk

The Pedigree trademark, email and website addresses, are the sole and exclusive properties of Pedigree Group Limited, used under licence in this publication.

**EDITOR** COLIN MITCHELL
**ASSISTANT EDITOR** DANIEL TYLER
**DESIGN** JONATHAN FINCH

SHOOT
.CO.UK

# CONTENTS

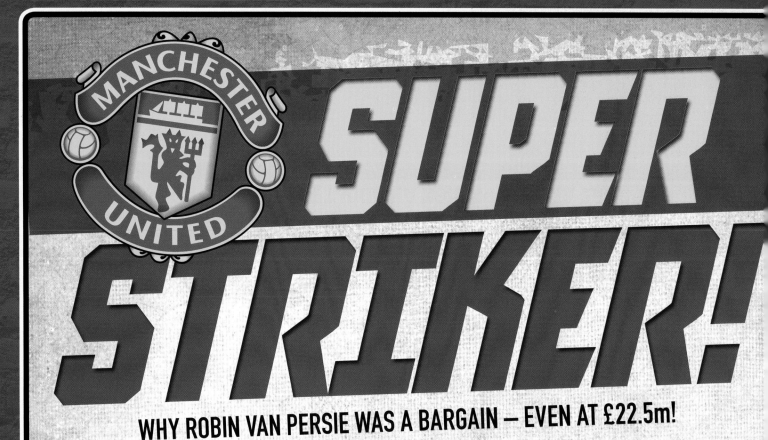

# SUPER STRIKER!

## WHY ROBIN VAN PERSIE WAS A BARGAIN — EVEN AT £22.5m!

Holland striker Robin van Persie cost Manchester United a staggering £22.5m in summer 2012.

But it was money well spent by Old Trafford boss Sir Alex Ferguson as the Holland hit-man scored 26 league goals in his debut season with the Red Devils.

Arsenal fans were gutted to lose their captain and top scorer – especially to one of their biggest Premier League rivals.

But Ferguson – who had always tried to avoid big transfer fees for older players – knew that it was going to be money well spent when he grabbed a player then aged 28.

Van the Man didn't let his new boss down and was soon among the goals as United shot to the top of the league. Here's what he thought about his new life in the north west…

### WAS IT EASY TO SETTLE IN AT MANCHESTER UNITED?

"From day one they made me feel at home. Every day I worked on new things and I have become aware of little things and small details that make me better. I am seeing things I didn't see for a long time."

### HOW DID FORMER COACH RENE MEULENSTEEN, ANOTHER DUTCHMAN, HELP?

"He is one of the best coaches in the world and every training session was unique. We knew exactly what he expected and he prepared us well."

### YOU SOON GOT TO 20 GOALS TOO!

"It should have been more as there were at least four or five early on that I shouldn't have missed. I had more chances than just one chance and one goal in some games."

### CAN YOU PLAY AS LONG AS RYAN GIGGS AND PAUL SCHOLES?

"I always thought I would go on until very late, but then I see these boys and how they can still run the show. Giggsy is incredible. I just can't imagine the day when I stop playing and it's all over because I know I'll miss the buzz so much."

### WHAT WAS IT LIKE LINKING UP WITH WAYNE ROONEY?

"He is a big player and a good all-rounder, who can score goals, provide assists and make nice runs. He has everything."

EXTRA TIME — Robin Van Persie refused to celebrate when he scored for Manchester United against Arsenal in November 2012.

## WHAT ARE YOU LIKE ON THE PITCH?

"I'm not a big shouter but I can be direct. If someone does something wrong I can give it to them straight – otherwise no one would take me seriously!"

## AND YOU HAVE PLAYED PLENTY OF GAMES OVER THE PAST SEASON!

"I'm used to playing games every few days. I like it because I get into a rhythm. When you don't play for more than a week, it can take you ten to 15 minutes to start because you're missing that rhythm. I love the buzz, drama and excitement of the big games but I know that the smaller games are very important, too — they're the ones that make you champions."

## WHAT HE'S WON

**UEFA Cup:** 2002
**Dutch Football Talent of the Year:** 2002

**FA Cup:** 2005
**Community Shield:** 2004
**Player of the Season:** 2009, 2012
**Premier League Golden Boot:** 2012
**PFA Players' Player of the Year:** 2012
**PFA Fans' Player of the Year:** 2012
**Football Writers' Footballer of the Year:** 2012

**Premier League Champions:** 2013
**Premier League Golden Boot:** 2013

## ❯ FACT FILE
### ROBIN VAN PERSIE

**Position:** Striker
**Birth date:** August 6, 1983
**Birth place:** Rotterdam, Holland
**Height:** 1.83m (6ft)
**Clubs:** Feyenoord, Arsenal, Manchester United
**International:** Holland

## ❯ WHAT HIS BOSS SAYS...

"He is absolutely relishing his new challenge. He is the right player, at the right club, at the right time. He has a winning mentality, but as he points out, it is one that goes right through the squad."

**Sir Alex Ferguson,**
*Retired Man United manager*

**EXTRA TIME** Van Persie scored 100 goals in his first 239 appearances for Arsenal, the 17th Gunner to pass the century mark.

SHOOT ANNUAL 2014 **7**

# MESSI MILESTONES

LIONEL MESSI IS NOT ONLY THE GREATEST PLAYER ON THE PLANET, HE'S ALSO DESTINED TO BE ONE OF THE BIGGEST FOOTBALL LEGENDS OF ALL-TIME. HERE ARE JUST SOME OF THE AMAZING MILESTONE IN HIS INCREDIBLE CAREER!

**1987** **June 24:** Born in Rosario, Argentina.

Messi as a child (back left)

**1998** Moved to Spain to join Barcelona's youth academy.

**2003** **November 16:** Senior debut for Barca in friendly v Porto

**2004** **October 16:** La Liga debut v Espanyol

**2005** **May 1:** First senior goal for Barcelona, v Albacete

**September:** Camp Nou contract extended to 2014

Wins FIFA Under-20 World Cup

**2006**

**March 1:** First international goal, v Croatia

**February 29:** First international hat-trick, v Switzerland

**June 9:** International hat-trick, v Brazil

**2008** Won Olympic Gold

Won third consecutive Young Player of the Year award

**February 27:** 100th game for Barcelona

EXTRA TIME Messi is under contract to Barcelona until 2018 – with a 250m euro (£203m) buyout clause in his deal.

## 2009

First Ballon d'Or win

UEFA Club Footballer of the Year

**December 19:** Scored winner against Estudiantes in Club World Cup

## 2010

Second Ballon d'Or win

**January 17:** 100th goal for Barcelona, against Sevilla

**April 6:** Scored four goals for first time; against Arsenal in Champions League

## 2011

Third Ballon d'Or win

Scored 200th goal for Barcelona

## 2012

Fourth Ballon d'Or win

**March 20:** Became Barca's all-time leading scorer

**December 9:** Hit 86th goal of calendar year, a new world best

## 2013

**February:** Scored 300th goal for Barca, part of a double against Granada

**March:** Set new world best by scoring in 17 consecutive La Liga games

### >> LEO'S GOAL TRAIL

**MESSI'S TALLY OF GAMES AND GOALS IN LA LIGA**

| Season | Games | Goals |
|---|---|---|
| 2004-05 | 7 | 1 |
| 2005-06 | 17 | 6 |
| 2006-07 | 26 | 14 |
| 2007-08 | 28 | 10 |
| 2008-09 | 31 | 23 |
| 2009-10 | 35 | 34 |
| 2010-11 | 33 | 31 |
| 2011-12 | 37 | 50 |
| 2012-13 | 32 | 46 |

**EXTRA TIME** Messi is believed to earn around 16m euros (£13.6m) a year. He is thought to have lots of incentive payments in his deal.

SHOOT ANNUAL 2014  **9**

# FERGIE BY NUMBERS

He's arguably the best football manager ever. He is certainly No.1 as far as the Premier League is concerned. And following the announcement of his retirement at the end of 2012–13 we look back in numbers at the life of Man United legend Sir Alex Ferguson.

## 13
THE NUMBER OF PREMIER LEAGUE TITLES HE WON AS BOSS OF THE RED DEVILS

## 4
CLUBS HE WAS IN CHARGE OF: EAST STIRLINGSHIRE, ST. MIRREN, ABERDEE AND MAN UNITED!

## 10
GAMES IN CHARGE OF SCOTLAND'S NATIONAL TEAM IN 1985–86 WHEN HE STEPPED IN FOLLOWING THE DEATH OF JOCK STEIN

## 3
SCOTTISH PREMIER TITLES WON WITH ABERDEEN

## 4
SCOTTISH CUPS WITH THE DONS

## 2
UEFA CUP WINNERS' CU VICTORIES, ONE AT ABERDE THE OTHER AT UNITED. PL TWO UEFA SUPER CUPS, O AT EACH CLUB

# 2

CHAMPIONS LEAGUE
VICTORIES THANKS TO
WINS OVER BAYERN
MUNICH AND CHELSEA

# 11

TIMES PREMIER
LEAGUE MANAGER OF
THE SEASON

# 27

MANGER OF THE
MONTH AWARDS
IN ENGLAND'S
TOP-FLIGHT

# 1500

GAMES IN CHARGE
OF MAN UNITED
BETWEEN NOVEMBER
1986 AND MAY 2013

# 2155

MATCHES AS A
MANAGER, HAVING
KICKED OFF HIS
CAREER AS A GAFFER
IN JUNE 1974

# 49

TROPHIES DURING
HIS TIME AS A BOSS
MAKE HIM THE MOST
SUCCESSFUL BRITISH
MANAGER OF ALL-TIME

# 3

MAJOR PERSONAL
HONOURS FOR HIS
WORK IN FOOTBALL:
OBE (1983), CBE (1995)
AND KNIGHTED IN 1999

# 4

LEAGUE MANAGERS'
ASSOCIATION MANAGER
OF THE YEAR AWARDS

# THE GREAT FOOTBALL QUIZ

You think you know nearly everything there is to know about football? Here's your chance to test that knowledge in our tough three-part quiz. You'll find some of the answers in this Annual.

## PART 1
### PLAYERS

**QUESTION 1**

Which teenage striker did Man United buy from Everton for £25.6m in 2004?

**QUESTION 2**

Who is the tallest Englishman to play in the Premier League?

**QUESTION 5**

Which team was Damien Duff's first in England?

**QUESTION 3**

What nationality is Hugo Rodallega?

**QUESTION 4**

Name the only Omani keeper to play in the Premier League.

**QUESTION 7**

Against which team did Steven Gerrard earn his 100th cap for England?

**QUESTION 8**

West Ham keeper from Bolton Wanderers.

**QUESTION 6**

From which team did Manchester City sign midfielder David Silva?

## QUESTION 9

Arsenal's all-time record goal scorer.

## QUESTION 10

Everton midfielder who was their record signing.

## QUESTION 11

Stoke City's former Ipswich striker who plays for the Republic of Ireland.

## QUESTION 14

Republic of Ireland winger who cost Sunderland just £350,000 in 2011.

## QUESTION 12

Norwich City and England keeper who started his career at Cambridge United.

## QUESTION 13

Argentina winger at Newcastle United.

## QUESTION 17

Southampton's England-Under 21 defender from Crystal Palace.

## QUESTION 15

Tottenham's Cameroon left back.

## QUESTION 16

Chelsea's £23.5m midfield maestro from Spain.

## QUESTION 18

Former Rotherham striker nicknamed Alf at Reading.

## QUESTION 19

QPR's record buy in January 2013 transfer window.

## QUESTION 20

Swansea City's hot-shot striker signed from Rayo Vallecano in 2012.

# SPOT THE BOSS!

All managers would love a bargain buy player, someone they can pick up on the cheap and turn into a hero. It's not easy finding those stars of tomorrow so many coaches and scouts sneak into games to watch their transfer targets. Can you find the SIX top managers who have hidden in this crowd?

## FACES IN THE CROWD

### ANDRE VILLAS-BOAS
### BRENDAN RODGERS
### PAOLO DI CANIO

**EXTRA TIME** During his time at Porto Andre-Villas Boas, now Tottenham manager, won the Portuguese league title, Portugal Cup and Europa League, all in 2011. The previous year his side won the Portugal Super Cup.

**HARRY REDKNAPP**  **SIR ALEX FERGUSON**  **DAVID MOYES**

# GOLDEN BALLS

DAVID BECKHAM FINALLY HUNG UP HIS FOOTBALL BOOTS LAST SEASON JUST DAYS AFTER HIS 38TH BIRTHDAY. HIS FAVOURITE SHIRT NUMBER WAS TWENTY-THREE, SO HERE ARE 23 MEMORIES ABOUT THE PLAYER CHRISTENED BY HIS WIFE AS GOLDENBALLS!

Becks made 115 England appearances, making him the country's most-capped outfield player.

Becks and Victoria "Posh Spice" Adams were married in July 1999 and were pictured sitting on golden thrones.

He played for some of the biggest teams around in Manchester United, Real Madrid, AC Milan, Paris Saint-Germain and at LA Galaxy.

Becks made his England debut on September 1, 1996 and played his last international when he came on as a sub against Belarus on October 14, 2009.

The midfielder won league titles in England, Spain, USA and France!

The first of his 17 England goals, which included five penalties, came in a 2-0 World Cup finals win against Colombia on June 26, 1998. It was a trademark curling 30-yard free-kick.

Beckham became public enemy No. 1 when he was sent off in the 1998 World Cup finals for kicking out at Argentina's Diego Simeone — and England lost in a penalty shoot-out.

He's not afraid to laugh at himself and crack a few jokes: he jokingly refused to answer someone's phone during a Press conference because it wasn't made by one of his sponsors.

Becks never forgets his roots and on visits back home is often spotted in his favourite East End pie and mash shop.

He restored his idol status with an amazing free-kick against Greece at Old Trafford that ensured England's passage to the 2002 World Cup finals.

There were many fashion statements — but would you have been brave enough to wear that sarong like he did?

And don't forget the hairstyles! Plaits, quiff, Mohican, shaved, long... you name it, he's probably done it!

Tattoos... where do we start? Maybe we should credit him with boosting the craze of body art. He's certainly had some interesting pieces.

All the cash he earned at PSG was given to charity. We know he's loaded but it was still around £3.5m!!!!!

EXTRA TIME  Beckham was sold by Manchester United to Real Madrid in summer 2003 for almost £25m.

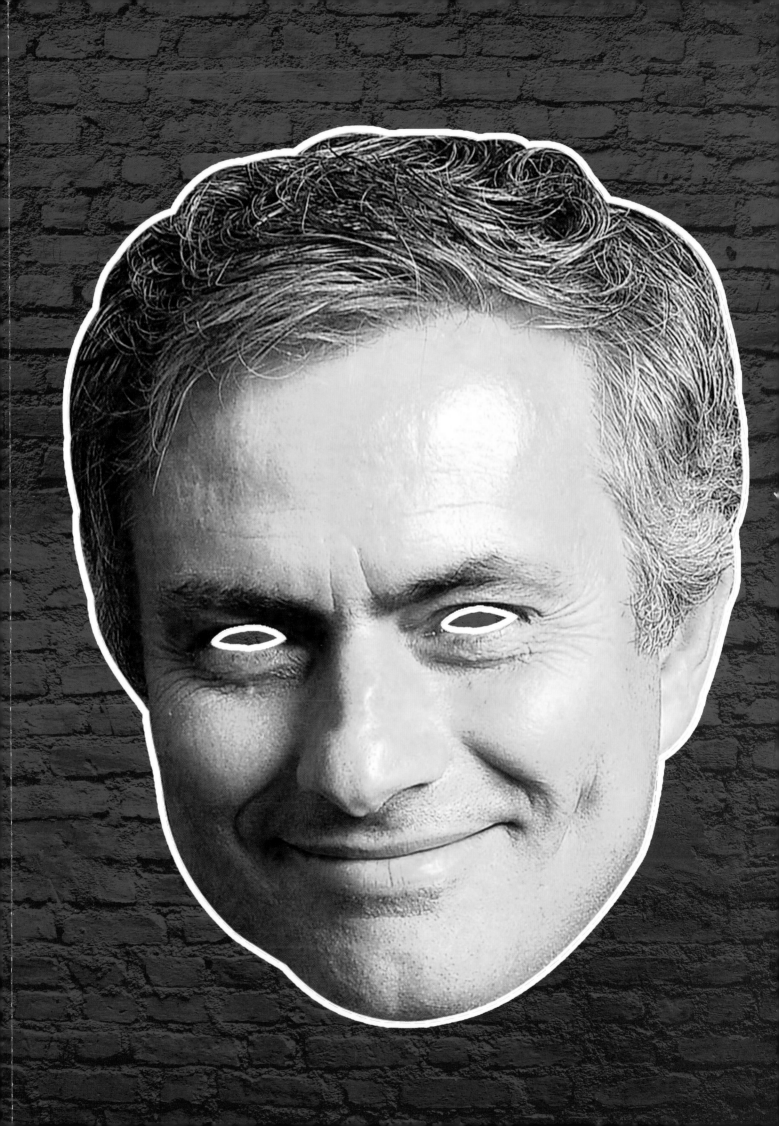

ATTACH ELASTIC
WITH TAPE HERE

ATTACH ELASTIC
WITH TAPE HERE

And he received a total of nine red cards during his career, including two for England and one just eight minutes after coming on as a sub for PSG in one of his final games.

He's not got it right every time — he once turned up to an England Press conference in an adidas hat when the national side's kit was sponsored by Umbro.

Becks was England captain for six years, covering 58 games.

Following the player's retirement, Prime Minster David Cameron Tweeted: "David Beckham has been an outstanding footballer throughout his career. Not only that, he has been a brilliant ambassador for this country, not least if we remember all the work he did in helping us win London 2012."

Posh and Becks have so far got four children: sons Brooklyn, Romeo and Cruz and daughter Harper.

The Londoner was part of the team that ensured the Olympic Games arrived in the capital in 2012. He wasn't so lucky in trying to get the World Cup finals.

He became even more famous through his many sponsorship deals, which included adidas, Brylcreem, Gillette, Pepsi... and those adverts where he posed in his underpants!

We've not seen the end of him! He's already an ambassador for Chinese football and Sky Sports, and is set for an important role at the Football Association.

He received the Order of the British Empire, OBE, on June 13, 2003.

**EXTRA TIME** Mr and Mrs Beckham are estimated to have a personal fortune which is worth in excess of £190m.

SHOOT ANNUAL 2014 **17**

# A FEW WORDS FROM...

## JAMES MILNER
### MANCHESTER CITY AND ENGLAND

### IT'S TRUE

Milner has played more than 100 games for Aston Villa, Newcastle and Man City

## HOW IMPORTANT IS IT TO THE CLUB TO PLAY IN THE CHAMPIONS LEAGUE?

"You play in this to play against the top teams and we know we can beat anyone on our day. It's really important that players get that experience and is a huge confidence boost. There are challenges that you just won't get away with in the Premier League."

## WHAT'S IT LIKE WHEN MANCHESTER CITY HAVE SUFFERED A DEFEAT?

"We don't need anyone to tell us if we have played well or not. We have a dressing room full of international players. We are a squad of winners and we work hard in training to get back to the level we should be. It's how you bounce back that's important. The drive is to win as many medals as you can."

## YOU STARTED AT LEEDS, TELL US A BIT ABOUT THE CLUB...

"I enjoyed every minute there, I am a Leeds lad, a Leeds fan and maybe one day I will go back. Never say never. My mum and dad had season tickets for years but gave them up when I left because they always come to watch me. My uncle and mates are fans too."

## WHAT WAS IT LIKE HAVING MARIO BALOTELLI AT MANCHESTER CITY?

"I miss him, to tell you the truth. He was crazy. It was like having a 12-year-old in the dressing room but he was harmless. The trick with Mario was to keep him busy."

## WE'VE HEARD YOU ARE GOOD AT OTHER SPORTS TOO...

"I was a wicket-keeper, who opened the batting. I might get back into it once I've finished with the football. I first played golf when I was 15 or 16. The best course I've done?" he pauses. "Pebble Beach in California. I pulled a few favours to get on it while I was on holiday three years ago.

## WHAT WAS IT LIKE WINNING AT MAN UNITED LAST SEASON?

"Every derby is a massive one, we wanted to put in a performance. We deserved the win at what is always a tough place to visit. It was a great result. We were the better team, worked hard and gave them few chances."

## FACT FILE
### JAMES PHILIP MILNER
**Position:** Midfielder
**Birth date:** January 4, 1986
**Birth place:** Leeds
**Height:** 1.76m (5ft 9in)
**Clubs:** Leeds United, Swindon (loan), Newcastle United, Aston Villa, Man City
**International:** England

**HE'S A WINNER!** Milner was the PFA Young Player of the Year in 2010. He was an FA Cup winner with Manchester City in 2011 and helped them lift the Premier League and Community Shield in 2012. He was also named in the PFA Premier League Team of the Year for 2010.

**EXTRA TIME** Milner's ability to play in a number of positions has made him a valuable squad member for club and country. He is regarded as a winger who can play on both sides – but also operates in centre midfield, as a striker or right back!

**BOSS ARSENE WENGER GOT SOME STICK LAST SEASON, DIDN'T HE?**

"He has built a legacy and changed everything since he came here. He brought total football to Arsenal, the passing game. He showed great faith in me when I was young and stuck with me after injury. There is no question that he is the right man for the job."

**HOW DIFFICULT WAS IT TO BE OUT FOR A LONG TIME WITH INJURY?**

"Obviously you start to question yourself as to whether you can get back to the level you were at before. I missed so much football I just need to work hard and get back to that level."

**DOES IT HELP PLAYING FOR ENGLAND WITH THE LIKES OF GERRARD AND LAMPARD?**

"To play with them is a dream. That they keep going is testatment to them. Ten years at the top is something I want to do."

**HOW DO YOU FEEL WHEN PLAYING FOR YOUR COUNTRY?**

"People say players are no longer bothered about wearing the England shirt. But for me it's the pinnacle of my job because club rivalries go out of the window and the entire nation comes together behind you — it's the best feeling. I want to captain Arsenal and I want to captain England."

**HOW DO YOU SEE YOUR CAREER PROGRESSING?**

"I'm not where I want to be yet. I want to work on my right foot and my long passing. I like to pick the ball up and run at players and drive the team on. I have been at the club since I was nine and in the first team from a young age. I would like to captain the club. I am not ready yet, but one day…"

**WHAT ABOUT THE TEAM'S MAIN TARGETS?**

"Our aim every season is to challenge for the Premier League. We know how desperate the fans are for a trophy and the players want silverware too. The likes of Manchester United go away and win games and leave you thinking, they keep winning and winning.' We also have to improve our record against the big teams. If you want to become champions you have to beat those sides."

> **IT'S TRUE**
> Wilshere was the PFA Young Player of the Year and Arsenal Player of the Season, both in 2011. He is also the tenth youngest player to turn out for England.

## FACT FILE

**JACK ANDREW GARRY WILSHERE**

Position: Midfielder
Birth date: January 1, 1992
Birth place: Stevenage, Hers
Height: 1.75m (5ft 9in)
Clubs: Arsenal, Bolton (loan)
International: England

**GUNNING FOR IT!** Arsenal used to be noted for their contingent of French players but Wilshere is part of a growing England and UK presence at the Emirates Stadium. England midfielder Wilshere, along with fellow international winger Alex Oxlade-Chamberlain, defenders Keiran Gibbs and Carl Jenkinson, plus forward Theo Walcott, have all pledged their futures to Arsenal. The Gunners have also handed a new deal to Welshman Aaron Ramsey and there are also a number of young England players coming through their reserves.

**EXTRA TIME** Former England captain Alan Shearer has predicted that Wilshere will one day skipper the Three Lions. Shearer made 63 appearances for the national side and captained his country 34 times.

SHOOT ANNUAL 2014　19

# THE SPECIAL

## 10 FACTS YOU NEED TO KNOW ABOUT JOSE MOURINHO

### FACT 1

He was born in Setubal, Portugal, on January 16, 1963 and went to University in Lisbon before he started playing as a midfielder in lower league football.

### FACT 2

Mourinho was a PE teacher before he became interpreter to Sir Bobby Robson when the former England manager was boss at Sporting Lisbon.

### FACT 3

He followed Sir Bobby to Porto and then Barcelona, watching and learning his coaching methods. Mourinho stayed with Barca when Robson left to join Newcastle United.

### FACT 4

He moved into management with Benfica for just under three months and was with Uniao de Leiria for nine months before taking over at Porto in 2002.

### FACT 5

In just over two years with Porto he lifted the Portuguese league title twice (2003, 2004), the Portugal Cup and Supercup (both 2003), UEFA Cup (2003) and Champions League (2004).

### FACT 6

His success in Portugal earned Mourinho the chance to become Chelsea manager in 2004, where he called himself "The Special One." He was certainly that as he won the Premier League twice (2005, 2006), the FA Cup (2007), League Cup (2005, 2007) and Community Shield (2005).

**EXTRA TIME** After leaving Real Madrid by "mutual agreement" Jose Mourinho returned to Chelsea as manager in June 2103. His four-year deal at Stamford Bridge is believed to have made him the Premier League's highest-paid boss.

# ONE

## FACT 7

Despite his success at Stamford Bridge, Mourinho fell out with club owner Roman Abramovich and left in September 2007. Nine months later he became boss of Inter Milan.

## FACT 8

In two years with the Italians Mourinho twice won Serie A (2009, 2010), the Italian Cup (2010), Italian Supercup (2008) and the Champions League (2010).

## FACT 9

Next stop for Mourinho was Real Madrid where he won La Liga (2012), Copa del Rey (2011) and the Spanish Supercup (2012).

## FACT 10

When Mourinho lifted the Champions League with Inter he became only the third manager in football history to win the trophy with two different teams. He was only the fourth coach to win league titles in at least four different countries (Portugal, England, Italy, Spain).

YOU CAN BE THE SPECIAL ONE! **DON'T FORGET TO MAKE YOUR MOURINHO MASK, GIVEN AWAY WITH THIS ANNUAL!**

# THE GREAT FOOTBALL QUIZ

You think you did well with Part 1 and the questions about players? Two more sections to go…and our second challenge is all about…

## PART 2
### TEAMS

**QUESTION 21**

Which team has won the most top-flight league titles in England?

..............................................................

**QUESTION 22**

The team in the Championship that has twice been European Champions…

..............................................................

**QUESTION 25**

The last team to win the FA Cup at the old Wembley in 2000.

..............................................................

**QUESTION 23**

1862

The English league team known as the Magpies — that isn't Newcastle United!

..............................................................

**QUESTION 24**

They are known as The Grecians but they don't play in Greece!

..............................................................

**QUESTION 26**

English club to win the European Cup FIVE times.

..............................................................

**QUESTION 27**

The team who used to play at Highbury before the ground was demolished.

..............................................................

**QUESTION 28**

Sky Sports TV pundit Matt Le Tissier played for this team for his entire career.

..............................................................

**QUESTION 29**

They played at the Victoria Ground before moving to the Britannia Stadium in 1997.

.............................................................

**QUESTION 30**

The side that took 44 years between winning the old First Division and then lifting the Premier League title.

.............................................................

**QUESTION 31**

Club that removed a pensioner from their crest in 1952 and now have a lion in their badge.

.............................................................

**QUESTION 34**

The two sides who would compete in an East Anglian derby.

.............................................................

**QUESTION 32**

South London club known as The Lions.

.............................................................

**QUESTION 33**

The club who play the Black Country derby against Wolves.

.............................................................

**QUESTION 37**

HOLTE END THE 12TH MAN

Their home fans are housed in the famous Holte End.

.............................................................

**QUESTION 35**

Club that returned to the Football League in 2006 after a 44-year break.

.............................................................

**QUESTION 36**

The side that used to have Borough in their team but ditched the word in 2010 — although their nickname is still Boro!

.............................................................

**QUESTION 39**

The Rokermen who became Black Cats.

.............................................................

**QUESTION 40**

First team from outside of England to play in the Premier League.

.............................................................

**QUESTION 38**

North London derby participants who play in white.

.............................................................

# MY FAVOURITE PLAYER

**Big names nominate the team-mates and opposition stars they admire...**

## DANIEL STURRIDGE
### LIVERPOOL AND ENGLAND

"He gives Liverpool more pace and strength in the attack. He has the strength to hold the ball. It looks a good decision to bring him in."

**NOMINATED BY:**
**Jamie Carragher,**
*Former Liverpool and England defender*

## LEIGHTON BAINES
### EVERTON AND ENGLAND

"If Bainesy left I would probably cry because he's the guy you can always count on. He's going to give you eight out of ten every week. He somehow creates so much for this team from the left-back position, which is very rare."

**NOMINATED BY:**
**Tim Howard,** *Everton and USA keeper*

## GARETH BALE
### TOTTENHAM AND WALES

"He is not just a left winger. He can play in various positions, up front and on the right. He can go far in the game and has a good attitude as well."

**NOMINATED BY:**
**Ryan Giggs,**
*Manchester United and former Wales*

 **EXTRA TIME** Tim Howard has played more than 300 games for Everton since joining them from Manchester United. The USA star arrived on a season-long loan to Goodison Park at the start of 2006 but signed in a £3m deal in February 2007.

## SANTI CAZORLA
### ARSENAL AND SPAIN

"Santi Cazorla has definitely stood out – he's like the conductor of the team. He's in my Dream Team which is scoring me points as well!"

**NOMINATED BY:**
**Theo Walcott,**
*Arsenal and England forward*

## HATEM BEN ARFA
### NEWCASTLE AND FRANCE

"He's a player in a different class. I have known him a long time and I know what it is possible for him to do on the pitch."

**NOMINATED BY:**
**Yohan Cabaye,**
*Newcastle and France midfielder*

## ROBIN VAN PERSIE
### MAN UNITED AND HOLLAND

"He's a fantastic player. He's been a great addition to the team, scoring goals, and he's great to play with."

**NOMINATED BY:**
**Wayne Rooney,**
*Man United and England striker*

## JUAN MATA
### CHELSEA AND SPAIN

"He gives everything, every game. He runs hard and is a very creative player, making a lot of chances and scoring his fair share of goals."

**NOMINATED BY:**
**Daniel Sturridge,** *Liverpool and England striker*

**EXTRA TIME** Midfielder Juan Mata was a World Cup-winner with Spain in 2010 and two years later helped his country to victory in the European Championships. He signed for Chelsea from Valencia in summer 2011 for £23.5m.

SHOOT ANNUAL 2014   **25**

## PAPISS CISSE

### NEWCASTLE AND SENEGAL

**IT'S TRUE**

During his time at Frieburg, Cisse set a new record for an African playing in the Bundesliga when he scored 22 goals in 2010-11.

NEWCASTLE

**YOU HAVE SCORED SOME AMAZING GOALS, WHAT DOES IT FEEL LIKE GETTING THEM?**

"To be honest any goal, no matter how great or bad is the best feeling. There is a feeling that explodes inside you. As soon as the ball hits the back of the net it is a goal and I am happy."

**WERE YOU DISAPPOINTED TO SEE YOUR INTERNATIONAL TEAM-MATE DEMBA BA LEAVE NEWCASTLE?**

"I have known him for years and have always got along with him. He was one of the reasons I joined the club and he explained the great atmosphere here. Now there is more responsibility on my shoulders and I relish it."

**DIDN'T YOU HAVE A CHANCE TO JOIN OTHER CLUBS?**

"There were other English sides interested but Newcastle offered a unique opportunity. I knew this was the right club for me. I knew it was a great club when I arrived and I want to help it achieve the history it deserves."

**WHAT AMBITIONS DID YOU HAVE AS A YOUNGSTER?**

"As a child I used to imagine what it would be like to play in England. African players have been successful here and I want to become part of that success story. The Premier League is the best in the world, along with that in Spain."

**IT WASN'T EASY MAKING A CAREER IN FOOTBALL THOUGH, WAS IT?**

"I was playing football in the streets from an early age. I went to a good school but I had to wait until I joined the local football academy to get my first boots. I have never forgotten where I came from and help out my family with food, electricity and built them a large house. Football is everything to me and I don't know what I would have done without it."

**HOW MUCH PRESSURE IS THERE WEARING THAT FAMOUS NO.9 SHIRT?**

"I know it is a huge thing at Newcastle and a monumental honour for me. Alan Shearer set the bar very high and I must try to follow the path he has set. I need to be aware of what the shirt means. I am not trying to prove I am as good as him but to live up to what the shirt means. The only way I can do that is to play well and score goals."

> **FACT FILE**
>
> **PAPISS DEMBA CISSE**
>
> **Position:** Striker
> **Birth date:** June 3, 1985
> **Birth place:** Dakar, Senegal
> **Height:** **1.83m (6ft)**
> **Clubs:** Douanes Dakar, Metz, Cherbourg (loan), Chateauroux (loan), Freiburg, Newcastle United
> **International:** Senegal

**GOAL RUSH!** Cisse joined Newcastle from Bundesliga side Freiburg in January 2012 and then scored 13 goals in 14 Premier League games. Two of those came against Chelsea at Stamford Bridge and one of them, an incredible angled slice from outside of the penalty area, won Goal of the Season. The £9m striker's first nine goals in eight games made him Newcastle's most prolific scorer per game. He was also the club's fastest player to reach five goals.

**EXTRA TIME** Locally-born Alan Shearer is Newcastle United's all-time record goal scorer with 206 and the Premier League's best with 260. He joined the Geordies from Blackburn in 1996 for a then world record £15m and retired in 2006.

## HOW DO YOU GET THROUGH A TOUGH SEASON OR A BAD RESULT?

"You have to find a way mentally to be strong enough to move on. The attitude and camaraderie we have developed has been fantastic. Even when results didn't go our way we stuck together and fought for each other. That pulls you through."

## HOW IMPORTANT IS WINNING?

"Every time you get a result, on a Sunday or the beginning of the season, it makes for an easier Monday morning. It is one good result or one good performance and you have to build on that. You have to progress. In this league you seldom get a week off but there is plenty of time in the summer to relax."

## YOU HAD A TOUGH TIME AT VILLA BEFORE ESTABLISHING YOURSELF...

"It's been a bit up and down. There have been definitely some good and great times, but there have been some frustrating times as well. Villa were extremely loyal to me in terms of giving me a chance to come from the US to England and start my European career. It's about proving yourself to the manager day-in, day-out. I want to hear my name when the manager reads out the starting 11."

## WHAT'S IT LIKE BEING A KEEPER?

"You need your team-mates and to have them in front of you blocking shots and stopping crosses and tackling – doing all those things that go unnoticed that help me as a goalkeeper – is tremendous. All sorts of things go on in the box, there's shirt-pulling, pushing, shoving, stepping on toes, it all goes on during set plays and corners."

## DO KEEPERS NEED MORE PROTECTION?

"You try to fight it off, you just try to get on with it. You hope the ref sees it and gives a foul. It is a physical position and you have to be able to be brave, strong, commanding, and make your presence felt. There will be times when you come and you clean out the striker and get your blow in and there will be times when he gets his in and you are lying flat on your back and seeing stars. You have to be able to dust yourself off and go again."

**IT'S TRUE**

Guzan won both of Aston Villa's Player of the Year awards at the end of season 2012-13.

### > FACT FILE

**BRADLEY EDWIN GUZAN**

**Position:** Keeper
**Birth date:** September 9, 1984
**Birth place:** Illinois, USA
**Height:** **1.93m (6ft 4in)**
**Clubs:** Chicago Fire, Chivas, Aston Villa, Hull City (loan)
**International:** USA

**DID YOU KNOW?** Guzan is one of five USA keepers to have played in the Premier League. One of them, Brad Friedel, kept him out of the Villa side and then his route to the No.1 shirt was blocked by the arrival of Republic of Ireland shot-stopper Shay Given. Guzan was even released by the Villans in summer 2012 — only to sign on again within a month! He then kept Given out of the Villa side and made 36 Premier League appearances in 2012-13 and is currently No.2 for America, behind Everton's Tim Howard.

**EXTRA TIME** USA keeper Brad Friedel played 131 games for Villa between 2008-11 after joining them from Blackburn Rovers. He is the Villans' oldest-ever player, having turned out for them at 40 years and four days before leaving for Spurs.

SHOOT ANNUAL 2014 **27**

# TRANSFER TRAIL

This could be a tough task for you! We've listed eight top players and the teams they were with at the end of season 2012-13. We want you to write into the spaces provided the team they used to turn out for and their international side. We've made life a bit easier by listing the information you need...

## WAYNE ROONEY – MAN UNITED
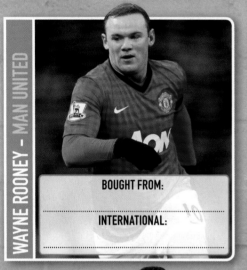
BOUGHT FROM:
...................................
INTERNATIONAL:
...................................

## STEVEN FLETCHER – SUNDERLAND
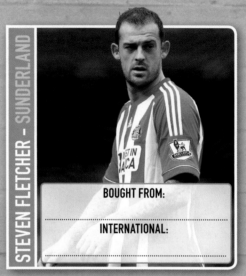
BOUGHT FROM:
...................................
INTERNATIONAL:
...................................

## YOHAN CABAYE – NEWCASTLE

BOUGHT FROM:
...................................
INTERNATIONAL:
...................................

## MOUSSA DEMBELE – TOTTENHAM

BOUGHT FROM:
...................................
INTERNATIONAL:
...................................

## SANTI CAZORLA – ARSENAL
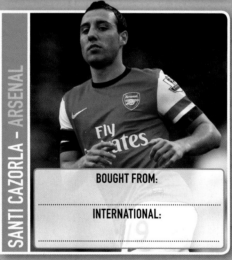
BOUGHT FROM:
...................................
INTERNATIONAL:
...................................

## RAMIRES – CHELSEA
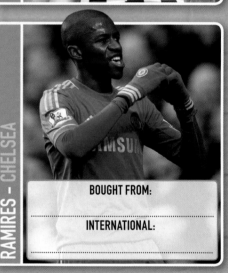
BOUGHT FROM:
...................................
INTERNATIONAL:
...................................

## SERGIO AGUERO – MAN CITY

BOUGHT FROM:
...................................
INTERNATIONAL:
...................................

## JOE ALLEN – LIVERPOOL
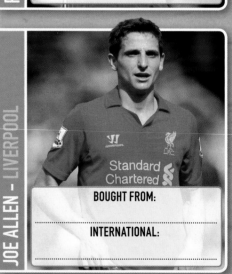
BOUGHT FROM:
...................................
INTERNATIONAL:
...................................

| TEAMS | INTERNATIONAL |
|---|---|
| FULHAM | ARGENTINA |
| LILLE | SCOTLAND |
| EVERTON | WALES |
| ATLETICO MADRID | FRANCE |
| SWANSEA CITY | ENGLAND |
| BENFICA | BRAZIL |
| WOLVES | BELGIUM |
| MALAGA | SPAIN |

**EXTRA TIME** Although they have won the Welsh Cup ten times, Swansea City's 2013 League Cup win was their first major trophy. They have also lifted the Football League Trophy twice (1994 and 2006) and twice been FA Cup semi-finalists.

# NAME THE PLAYERS!

Four players, four clues for each – and we want you to tell us who these Premier League stars are!

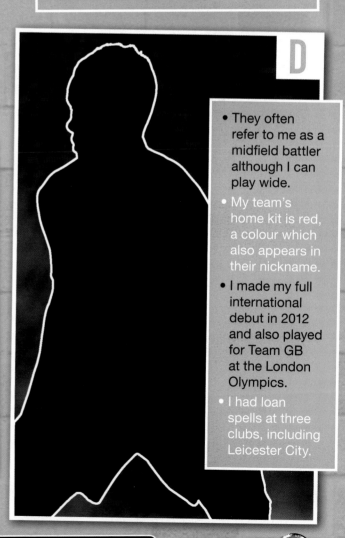

**A**

- I am a striker.
- I have played for Harry Rednapp at three different clubs.
- I scored a series of goals to set a Division Two scoring record.
- My international shirt and first-choice club shirt are both white.

**B**

- I am a central defender.
- I've captained both club and country.
- The club's colours are blue and international shirt white or red.
- Many of my friends call me by my initials.

**C**

- I play between the sticks and my first name sounds English – but I am not from England.
- My birthday is on Boxing Day.
- I've played for my country at all levels from Under-18 to senior, and have captained the side.
- My Premier League club bought me from Lyon in summer 2012 for almost £12m.

**D**

- They often refer to me as a midfield battler although I can play wide.
- My team's home kit is red, a colour which also appears in their nickname.
- I made my full international debut in 2012 and also played for Team GB at the London Olympics.
- I had loan spells at three clubs, including Leicester City.

**EXTRA TIME** The world's most expensive keeper was Gianluigi Buffon who cost Juventus £32.6m when they bought him from Parma in 2001. Since 1997 he has played more than 120 games for Italy and captained both club and country.

**SHOOT ANNUAL 2014** 29

# 150 YEARS OF

The Football Association is the ruling body for the game in England and in 2013 celebrated its 150th birthday.

The Association was formed on October 26, 1863 at the Freemason's Tavern in central London and is the oldest FA in the world.

The organisation's job is not to make a profit but to be responsible for looking after all aspects of football in the country, to make sure the game grows and that it is played to the rules.

## THE FA IN NUMBERS

**7,000,000 people** play football at grassroots level

**2,000,000 play** every week

**1,100 leagues** in England

**115,000 teams**

**29,000 clubs**

**30,000,000 tickets sold each year to watch professional games**

**300,000 coaches**

**24 international sides from youth to senior, women and various disabilities**

**27,000 qualified referees**

**400,000 volunteers support the game**

**EXTRA TIME** The FA Cup is the oldest domestic football knockout competition in the world. The first final in 1871-72 was won by Wanderers who beat the Royal Engineers 1-0. Manchester United have won the most FA Cups, 11 in total.

# THE FA

① 1888: England
② 1890: Ireland
③ 1890: Scotland
④ 1890: Netherlands
⑤ 1891: Argentina
⑥ 1895: Belgium
⑦ 1897: Switzerland
⑧ 1900: Uruguay
⑨ 1901: Hungary
⑩ 1906: Paraguay
⑪ 1909: Romania
⑫ 1911: Austria
⑬ 1912: Peru
⑭ 1921: USA
⑮ 1921: Tunisia
⑯ 1921: Venezuela
⑰ 1924: Sweden
⑱ 1924: Bulgaria
⑲ 1925: Czechoslovakia
(1993: Czech Republic and Slovakia).
⑳ 1927: Greece
㉑ 1929: Spain
㉒ 1929: Italy
㉓ 1929: Denmark
㉔ 1932: France
㉕ 1933: Chile
㉖ 1936: USSR
㉗ 1937: Norway
㉘ 1937: Haiti
㉙ 1938: Portugal
㉚ 1943: Mexico
㉛ 1948: Colombia
㉜ 1956: Ghana
㉝ 1957: Ecuador
㉞ 1959: Brazil
㉟ 1959: Turkey
㊱ 1960: Ivory Coast
㊲ 1962: Algeria
㊳ 1962: Zambia
㊴ 1963: Germany
㊵ 1965: Japan
㊶ 1966: Mali
㊷ 1966: Nigeria
㊸ 1977: Australia
㊹ 1977: Bolivia
㊺ 1983: South Korea
㊻ 1988: Panama
㊼ 1992: Croatia
㊽ 1992: Ukraine
㊾ 2000: Bosnia
㊿ 2001: Russia
51 2006: Montenegro
52 2006: Serbia

## 125 YEARS OF THE FOOTBALL LEAGUE

The Football League, the world's original divisional competition, celebrated its 125th anniversary in 2013.

In 1888 founder William McGregor sent out a letter suggesting "ten or twelve of the most prominent clubs in England combine to arrange home-and-away fixtures each season."

That led to what we now have as the Premier League, Championship and Leagues One and Two – with scores of lesser divisions.

The first Football League season kicked-off on September 8, 1888.

Founder teams were Accrington, Aston Villa, Blackburn Rovers, Bolton Wanderers, Burnley, Derby County, Everton, Notts County, Preston North End, Stoke, West Bromwich Albion and Wolverhampton Wanderers.

This map shows when leagues around the world were set up.

EXTRA TIME — The first Football League in 1888-89 was won by Preston North End who went the whole of the season unbeaten. Arsenal are the only other side to complete a season without defeat, a feat they accomplished in 2003-04.

## STEVEN GERRARD
### LIVERPOOL AND ENGLAND

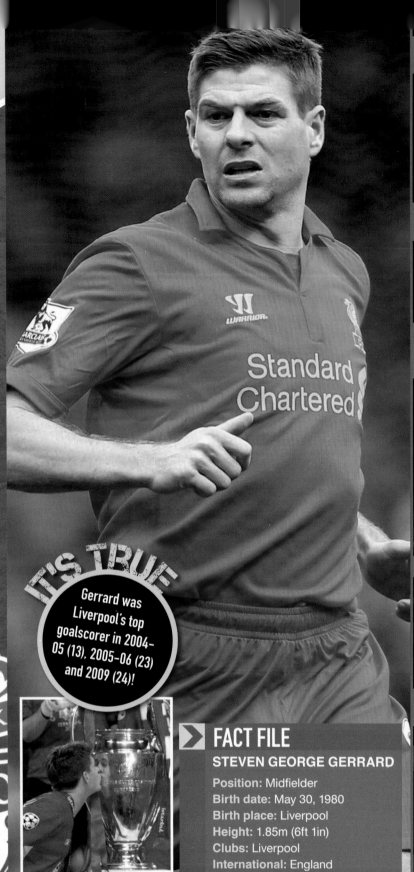

**IT'S TRUE**

Gerrard was Liverpool's top goalscorer in 2004–05 (13), 2005–06 (23) and 2009 (24)!

## WHAT POSITION DO YOU LIKE PLAYING BEST?

"If the manager says I am playing centre midfield or off the front man there is no massive difference to me. I'll play wherever the manager wants me to and not worry about it. If I play out of position and we get a win I still get the same buzz."

## WHAT ARE YOUR MOST MEMORABLE MOMENTS WITH LIVERPOOL?

"As captain when I have lifted trophies – the FA Cup and the European Cup. I still get a tingle about the Champions League Final [2005, against AC Milan]."

## BUT YOU REALLY DIDN'T ENJOY THE PENALTY SHOOT-OUT AGAINST GERMANY AT WORLD CUP 2006...

"It all happened so fast and I felt after the penalties that I'll be a bit more composed next time. It's massive pressure but we have to try and handle that. It's not like taking a normal penalty in practice, you have so much more responsibility. What you can do is be ready, not shy away from it and have the bottle to step up for another go, especially if you've missed one before."

## IS IT DIFFICULT PLAYING FOR ENGLAND?

"There is pressure and fear playing for England, but it doesn't help playing with fear. You must be relaxed, patient and the performance will come. You need to be aggressive, compact and tough, have that cutting edge."

## DO YOU ENJOY PLAYING FOR THE THREE LIONS?

"I love it. I've had a lot of lows with England but for me there's still an opportunity to go out on a high with England and that's the challenge. When we win we get a lot of credit, so when it doesn't go well we deserve criticism."

### FACT FILE
**STEVEN GEORGE GERRARD**

**Position:** Midfielder
**Birth date:** May 30, 1980
**Birth place:** Liverpool
**Height:** 1.85m (6ft 1in)
**Clubs:** Liverpool
**International:** England

**HE'S A WINNER!** Gerrard has won two FA Cups (2001, 2006), three League Cups (2001, 2003, 2012), two Community Shields (2001, 2006), a Champions League (2005), UEFA Cup (2001) and two UEFA Super Cups (2001, 2005). He was also Football Writers' Footballer of the Year (2009), PFA Players' Player of the Year (2006), PFA Young Player of the Year (2001), PFA Fans' Player of the Year (2001, 2009) and was also voted England Player of the Year (2007).

**EXTRA TIME** Gerrard made his England debut in May 2000. His first goal came in the stunning 5-1 World Cup 2002 qualifying victory in Germany in 2001. He played at World Cup 2006 and 2010 and Euro 2004 and 2012.

## JUAN MATA
### CHELSEA AND SPAIN

**IS IT TRUE YOU SIGNED FOR CHELSEA BECAUSE OF THE COLOUR OF THE TEAM'S SHIRTS?**

"From being a little boy my colour was always blue. I wanted to come to England to win trophies and that is why I accepted Chelsea's offer. It was a question of sporting achievement not money. I want the Premier League title and it is possible at Chelsea."

**WHAT WAS THE BIGGEST CHALLENGE WHEN YOU JOINED THE BLUES?**

"The physical side of the game. It's a different kind of football to Spain, more physical, a different pace, but when you have players around you like we have at Chelsea it makes things very easy."

**HOW HAVE YOU FOUND LIFE AT STAMFORD BRIDGE?**

"I have been given the chance to grow professionally at a big club. It is also important to me to grow as a person. To score in my first game gave me a lot of confidence and when you play with high quality players it is easier. I enjoy playing here. The aim is to do the best you can with any team. I want to play as many minutes as I can."

**YOU'VE PLAYED AT WEMBLEY A FEW TIMES, WHAT WAS THAT LIKE?**

"In my first season in England I won my first trophy with Chelsea there – the FA Cup – so it is a very special venue for me. Even when I was playing in Spain, I realised that Wembley was one of the most important football stadiums in the world because of its history staging the big matches and so many finals. My first match there was for Spain against England and then with Chelsea I really enjoyed the semi-finals and final of the FA Cup."

**YOU'VE WON TWO BIG TITLES WITH SPAIN, SO WHAT'S NEXT?**

"I cannot explain how happy I am for winning the Euros and scoring a goal in the final, I cannot ask for anything more. Hopefully we can repeat that triumph at the World Cup finals in Brazil in 2014. I have already enjoyed experiencing three major tournaments and my only goal is to keep being involved. When you are going to play in Brazil, the Maracana always comes to mind. It would be fantastic if we could reach the final there and win it."

**IT'S TRUE**
Mata cost Chelsea almost £23.5m from Valencia in August 2011.

## FACT FILE
### JUAN MANUEL MATA GARCIA

**Position:** Midfielder
**Birth date:** April 28, 1988
**Birth place:** Ocon de Villafranca, Spain
**Height:** 1.7m (5ft 7in)
**Clubs:** Real Madrid B, Valencia, Chelsea
**International:** Spain

**HE'S A WINNER!** Mata won the Copa del Rey with Valencia; a triple of FA Cup, Champions League and Fans' Player of the Year at the end of his first season with Chelsea; and was also a 2010 World Cup winner and 2012 European Championships winner with Spain.

**EXTRA TIME** Mata was persuaded to make the move to Chelsea by Spain team-mate Fernando Torres, who had arrived at Stamford Bridge from Liverpool six months earlier.

# THE GREAT FOOTBALL QUIZ

Here are your final 20 questions! You can check your scores at the back of the Annual to see if you are a transfer success or failure! Your questions cover all sorts of things football...

**QUESTION 41**

What was the final score in the League Cup Final of 2013

**QUESTION 42**

Name the Russia striker Reading signed in summer 2012 on a free transfer.

**QUESTION 45**

What's the name of Chelsea's Russian billionaire owner?

**QUESTION 43**

Newcastle bought a load of French players in the January 2012 transfer window. Which one came from Toulouse?

**QUESTION 44**

Who is the only player to score in all 21 years of the Premier League?

**QUESTION 46**

Which League One side knocked Liverpool out of the 2012–13 FA Cup and then drew Everton?

**QUESTION 47**

When Tony Pulis took over at Stoke City in 2006 it was his second time as manager. True or false?

**QUESTION 48**

Bristol Rovers are known by two nicknames, The Gas and...?

**QUESTION 49**

The Riverside is home to which north east club?

.....................

**QUESTION 50**

Who was Tottenham manager before Andre Villas-Boas?

.....................

**QUESTION 51**

Who scored more Premier League goals, Alan Shearer, Thierry Henry or Frank Lampard?

.....................

**QUESTION 54**

What nationality is Aston Villa keeper Brad Guzan?

.....................

**QUESTION 52**

Which team was the first to score 1,000 Premier League goals?

.....................

**QUESTION 53**

Who was the permanent manager of Sunderland before Martin O'Neill took over in December 2011?

.....................

**QUESTION 57**

The nationality of Liverpool striker Luis Suarez.

.....................

**QUESTION 55**

Which of the three newly promoted teams did best in the Premier League in season 2012-13?

.....................

**QUESTION 56**

Who were the 2013 Championship Champions?

.....................

**QUESTION 59**

From which team did Everton sign striker Nikica Jelavic?

.....................

**QUESTION 60**

Who was full-time England manager before Roy Hodgson?

.....................

**QUESTION 58**

Andy Cole, Alan Shearer, Jermain Defoe and Dimitar Berbatov all hold the same goal scoring record. What is it?

.....................

# TOP TEN LISTS

Goals, points, money - these are the best in the Premier League and the world!

## WORLD'S MOST VALUABLE CLUBS

(on revenues, previous rating in brackets)

| | | | |
|---|---|---|---|
| 1 (1) | Real Madrid | £414.7m | (433) |
| 2 (2) | Barcelona | £390.8m | (407) |
| 3 (3) | Man United | £320.3m | (331.4) |
| 4 (4) | B. Munich | £298.1m | (290.3) |
| 5 (5) | Chelsea | £261m | (228.6) |
| 6 (6) | Arsenal | £234.9m | (226.8) |
| 7 (12) | Man City | £231.1m | (153.2) |
| 8 (7) | AC Milan | £207.9m | (212) |
| 9 (9) | Liverpool | £188.7m | (183.6) |
| 10 (13) | Juventus | £158.1m | (139) |

## EUROPEAN FOOTBALL'S TOP SCORERS 2012-13

| | | |
|---|---|---|
| 1. | Lionel Messi (Barcelona) | 46 |
| 2. | Cristiano Ronaldo (Real Madrid) | 34 |
| 3. | Philipp Hosiner (A. Vienna) | 32 |
| 4. | Wilfried Bony (Vitesse) | 31 |
| 5= | Zlatan Ibrahimovic (PSG) | 29 |
| 5= | Edinson Cavani (Napoli) | 29 |
| 7. | Radamel Falcao (A. Madrid) | 28 |
| 8. | Graziano Pelle (Feyenoord) | 27 |
| 9= | Robin Van Persie (Man United) | 26 |
| 9= | Jackson Martinez (Porto) | 26 |
| 9= | Jonathan Soriano (Salzburg) | 26 |

## WORLD'S RICHEST FOOTBALLERS

(£millions, at end of 2012-13)

| | | |
|---|---|---|
| 1. | David Beckham *Paris Saint-Germain* | £175m |
| 2. | Lionel Messi *Barcelona* | £115m |
| 3. | Cristiano Ronaldo *Real Madrid* | £112m |
| 4. | Kaka *Real Madrid* | £66m |
| 5. | Ronaldhino *Athletico Mineiro* | £63m |
| 6. | Samuel Eto'o *Anzi Makhachkala* | £52m |
| 7. | Wayne Rooney *Manchester United* | £50m |
| 8. | Zlatan Ibrahimovic *Paris Saint-Germain* | £47m |
| 9. | Rivaldo *Sao Caetano* | £45m |
| 10. | Rio Ferdinand *Manchester United* | £42m |

## BARCLAYS PREMIER LEAGUE

### MOST POINTS

| | | |
|---|---|---|
| 1. | Man United | 1,752 |
| 2. | Arsenal | 1,522 |
| 3. | Chelsea | 1,477 |
| 4. | Liverpool | 1,395 |
| 5. | Tottenham | 1,158 |
| 6. | Aston Villa | 1,130 |
| 7. | Everton | 1,097 |
| 8. | Newcastle | 1,058 |
| 9. | Blackburn | 970 |
| 10. | Man City | 862 |

### MOST LEAGUE APPEARANCES

| | | |
|---|---|---|
| 1. | Ryan Giggs | 620 |
| 2. | David James | 572 |
| 3. | Frank Lampard | 553 |
| 4. | Gary Speed | 534 |
| 5. | Emile Heskey | 516 |
| 6. | Jamie Carragher | 509 |
| 7. | Phil Neville | 505 |
| 8. | Mark Schwarzer | 504 |
| 9. | Sol Campbell | 503 |
| 10. | Paul Scholes | 499 |

### MOST GOALS

| | | |
|---|---|---|
| 1. | Alan Shearer | 260 |
| 2. | Andy Cole | 189 |
| 3. | Thierry Henry | 176 |
| 4. | Frank Lampard | 164 |
| 5. | Robbie Fowler | 162 |
| 6. | Wayne Rooney | 156 |
| 7. | Michael Owen | 150 |
| 8. | Les Ferdinand | 150 |
| 9. | Teddy Sheringham | 147 |
| 10. | JF Hasselbaink | 129 |

**EXTRA TIME** The above Premier League figures, correct to the end of 2012-13, should change again next year with Ryan Giggs (Manchester United) and Frank Lampard (Chelsea) both agreeing new contracts and Wayne Rooney still playing.

# AROUND THE WORLD

Time to prove just how much you know about some of the biggest clubs on the planet – and where they are based! We've listed ten top teams and placed ten spots on the map of the world. All you have to do is tell us which team belongs where!

BORUSSIA DORTMUND ◯

SHAKHTAR DONETSK ◯

DC UNITED ◯

NAPOLI ◯

FLAMENGO ◯

BENFICA ◯

CELTIC ◯

CSKA ◯

PANATHINAIKOS ◯

ROSENBORG ◯

**EXTRA TIME** Napoli, ranked as the 15th most valuable football club in the world in terms of how much money they earn, play in the 60,000 capacity Stadio San Paolo. One of their most famous player is Diego Maradona (1984-91).

SHOOT ANNUAL 2014 · 37

# WHICH BALL?

The Premier League ball is fast and swerves so much that even the best of keepers can be fooled by its flight. Are you as smart – or smarter – than these shop-stoppers? Can you decide which of the balls in these Premier League games are the real ones?

## GAME ONE

## GAME TWO

**EXTRA TIME** Nike have been the official suppliers of the Premier League match ball since 2000-01. Before that Mitre produced balls for England's top-flight games. Rivals adidas produce balls for the World Cup and European Championship.

# GAME THREE

# GAME FOUR

| GAME ONE: ARSENAL v LIVERPOOL | THE CORRECT BALL IS: | |
| GAME TWO: QPR v MAN CITY | THE CORRECT BALL IS: | |
| GAME THREE: FULHAM v MAN UNITED | THE CORRECT BALL IS: | |
| GAME FOUR: EVERTON v LIVERPOOL | THE CORRECT BALL IS: | |

Check your answers on page 77

EXTRA TIME History books claims TWO balls were used during the 1930 FIFA World Cup Final! Argentina led 2-1 after 45 minutes using their ball. Uruguay used their ball in the second half and won 4-2. FIFA now decides which ball is used.

## ADAM JOHNSON
### SUNDERLAND AND ENGLAND

**IT'S TRUE**

Johnson scored as Sunderland won 3-0 at Newcastle in April 2013. As a boy, he was a Magpies fan.

### WHERE ON THE PITCH DO YOU PLAY BEST?

"I'm left footed but when I was growing up as a winger you could play either side. It's not really that different. I don't mind which side I play on. I actually do my best work down the right. As a lad I liked Ryan Giggs and David Ginola in his prime – he used to go past people fully, not just half a yard to get a cross in. Apart from Robben, Messi and Ribery not many actually go past people with skill."

### HOW DO YOU LIKE TO PLAY?

"I want to impress and excite the fans. That's the type of player I used to watch, people who attack, are skilful and take others on. I just play my own game and these days all top wingers play on opposite sides so they can come inside on their stronger foot."

### HAVE YOU EVER LACKED CONFIDENCE?

"I always believed in myself that I could do it but at Middlesbrough it was hard. Sometimes I think I should have left earlier as I had Stewart Downing in front of me. Everyone wants to start games and I am no different."

### DO YOU EVER GET TOO CONFIDENT?

"My family and my mates keep my feet on the ground. Everyone has always been like that around me if I get too carried away or anything like that. I tend to play better when I have pressure."

### WHAT WAS IT LIKE SCORING IN SUNDERLAND'S BIGGEST WIN AT NEWCASTLE IN 34 YEARS?

"I don't think there is a better way to win over the fans. To score any goal is an amazing feeling but it's even better against your arch-rivals at their ground. I've been trying to create goals and improve the defensive side of things. If that's what it takes to stay in the team I am prepared to do it."

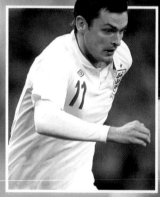

### ▶ FACT FILE

**ADAM JOHNSON**

**Position:** Winger
**Birth date:** July 14, 1987
**Birth place:** Sunderland
**Height:** 1.78m (5ft 10in)
**Clubs:** Middlesbrough, Leeds (loan), Watford (loan), Man City, Sunderland
**International:** England

**DID YOU KNOW?** Before he left Manchester City in summer 2012 for a £10m move to Sunderland, Johnson would have loved the shirt off his idol Ryan Giggs when he played against Manchester United – but the winger was so gutted at getting beaten he was "in a huff" and forgot to ask!

**EXTRA TIME** Johnson, an FA Youth Cup winner with Middlesbrough in 2004, made his debut for Boro when former England boss Steve McClaren was still club manager. He was sold to Man City in the January window 2010 for £8m.

## HOW DID YOU START PLAYING FOOTBALL?

"My friends and I used to play on a concrete basketball court. You had to play one-twos and that gave me a solution to everything."

## AND ISN'T ONE OF THOSE EARLY FRIENDS NOW A TEAM-MATE?

"I have known Jan Vertonghen since I was ten, when we played together. He told me a lot of good things about Spurs and I was happy to join them. All of the guys are very talented and a lot of them are young so there is a lot of potential in this team. I think they are already very good and can be even better."

## WHAT ABOUT THE PREMIER LEAGUE?

"There are no small teams in the league. Every opponent is a good player so you are tested week after week. I struggled to find my best position before I came to England but Martin Jol [at Fulham] put me in midfield and I was happy."

## YOU ARE ONE OF A NUMBER OF BELGIANS NOW PLAYING IN THE PREMIER LEAGUE. HOW HAS THAT HAPPENED?

"I don't know! I said to my team-mates I hope the whole team is in the Premier League, and now there are three or four more players here! Everybody is doing really well in England and I'm really proud of this. When you play against any other team where there is a Belgian, you want to win and I look forward to playing against Eden Hazard, Fellaini and the others."

## WHAT DO YOU DO WHEN YOU ARE NOT PLAYING?

"I don't watch much football, just the English competitions to be honest. Outside of football I like musicals in the West End. I've been to see *Jersey Boys* a few times and realised I knew most of the songs from when I was young. That was great."

### IT'S TRUE

Tottenham paid Fulham £15m to sign Dembele in August 2012. Exactly two years earlier he had cost the Cottagers just £5m from Dutch side AZ.

## FACT FILE

### MOUSA SIDI YAYA DEMBELE

**Position:** Midfielder
**Birth date:** July 16, 1987
**Birth place:** Wilrijk, Belgium
**Height:** 1.85m (6ft 1in)
**Clubs:** Germinal Beerschot, Willem II, AZ Alkmaar, Fulham, Tottenham
**International:** Belgium

**DID YOU KNOW?** Dembele won the Dutch Eredivisie in 2009 when he was playing for AZ Alkmaar. His club completed a Double that season by winning the Johan Cruyff Shield – a game between Holland's champions and the cup winners. AZ beat Heerenveen 5-1

**EXTRA TIME** Maria Huygens, Dembele's grandmother, used to play football in Belgium before the women's game became popular. She watches the Premier League on television and he reckons she recognises more players than he does!

# 11 QUESTIONS FOR IBRAHIMOVIC

## THE SWEDEN AND PARIS SAINT GERMAIN STRIKER, ONE OF THE HIGHEST PAID FOOTBALLERS IN THE WORLD, REVEALS HIS THOUGHTS...

**Q1** MESSI OR RONALDO?

For me Messi is natural, Ronaldo is a trained product.

**Q2** ON A SCALE OF ZERO TO TEN, HOW GOOD ARE YOU AS A FOOTBALLER?

10!

**Q3** DO YOU THINK YOU'RE UNDERRATED?

No, they know I'm good.

**Q4** WHAT'S YOUR BIGGEST WEAKNESS?

That I have to think long. Heading the ball.

**Q5** TOUGHEST DEFENDER YOU'VE FACED?

Paolo Maldini

**EXTRA TIME** Zlatan Ibrahimovic's £18m move from AC Milan to Paris Saint-Germain in summer 2012 brought his combined transfer fee moves to £171.1m, the largest total ever paid for one player.

## Q6 BEST COACH YOU'VE EVER HAD?

I've had many great coaches. I would put Capello and Mourinho in first position.

## Q7 HOW MUCH DO YOU WANT TO WIN THE CHAMPIONS LEAGUE?

A lot, but it doesn't mean anything because my career has been fantastic anyway.

## Q8 LONG HAIR OR SHORT HAIR FOR YOU?

Long hair because my strength is in my hair.

## Q9 HIP HOP, ROCK...

Reggae. That's for after the game you know, to enjoy.

## Q10 PARIS, BARCELONA, OR MILAN TO LIVE?

Milan.

## Q11 IF NOT A FOOTBALLER...

Lawyer. That's what my father wanted, but I really don't know.

### FACT FILE

**ZLATAN IBRAHIMOVIĆ**

**Position:** Striker
**Birth date:** October 3, 1981
**Birth place:** Malmo, Sweden
**Height:** 1.95m (6ft 5in)
**Clubs:** Malmo, Ajax, Juventus, Inter Milan, Barcelona, AC Milan, Paris Saint Germain
**International:** Sweden

### ▶ WHAT HIS BOSS SAYS...

"He is our captain and our best player. He's a really good player – a world-class player – and a country like Sweden can't afford not to have players like him in our team."

**Erik Hamren,** *Sweden manager*

**EXTRA TIME** Ibrahimovic's first season at PSG brought 35 goals in 46 games as his team won the French title for the first time since 1994. The Swede was Ligue 1's top scorer with 30 goals, the first player to reach that figure since 1990.

SHOOT ANNUAL 2014 **43**

# TRUE OR FALSE?

**Can you sort the football facts from the fiction? Answers at the back...**

BAAAAAA!

**1** Newcastle striker Papiss Cisse just loves a curry made with goat.

TRUE ☐ FALSE ☐

**2** Kevin Bond has been part of Harry Redknapp's backroom team at Portsmouth, Southampton, Tottenham and QPR.

TRUE ☐ FALSE ☐

**3** Bradford City, 2013 League Cup finalists, once spent two seasons in the Premier League.

TRUE ☐ FALSE ☐

**4** Scotland and Sunderland striker Steven Fletcher was born in Shropshire.

TRUE ☐ FALSE ☐

**5** Chelsea defender Cesar Azpilicueta is know as 'Dave' to his team-mates because they have trouble saying his name.

TRUE ☐ FALSE ☐

You don't know the power of the dark side!

**6** Defender Wayne Bridge, on loan last season at Brighton, is a massive Star Wars fans and has even dressed up as Darth Vader.

TRUE ☐ FALSE ☐

**7** Gareth Bale was great at all sports whilst at school and could have played cricket for Wales.

TRUE ☐ FALSE ☐

**8** Wigan Athletic's mascot used to be a labrador called Willie the Wonder dog.

TRUE ☐ FALSE ☐

**9** Former Arsenal forward Andrei Arshavin has designed women's clothing.

TRUE ☐ FALSE ☐

**10** Super sub Ole Gunnar Solskjaer scored a hat-trick for Man United in the last 12 minutes of a game against Nottingham Forest.

TRUE ☐ FALSE ☐

**EXTRA TIME** Almost 30 animals and birds take part in the annual football mascots race – won in 2012-13 by York City's Yorkie the Lion, ahead of Burton Albion's Bill Brewer with Oldham Athletic's Chaddy Owl third.

# WAVE THE FLAG!

Any footballer who turns out for his country is rightly proud.
Can you link the players on this page with their national side's flags?
We've given you a big help by putting the name of the countries with the flags.

**GEOFF CAMERON**
STOKE CITY
FLAG:

**KARIM BENZEMA**
REAL MADRID
FLAG:

**DEMBA BA**
CHELSEA
FLAG:

**ANDERS LINDEGAARD**
MANCHESTER UNITED
FLAG:

GERMANY

SENEGAL

USA

DENMARK

SWEDEN

SCOTLAND

FRANCE

BELGIUM

**STEVEN NAISMITH**
EVERTON
FLAG:

**MARCO REUS**
BORUSSIA DORTMUND
FLAG:

**JONAS OLSSON**
WEST BROM
FLAG:

**JAN VERTONGHEN**
TOTTENHAM HOTSPUR
FLAG:

**EXTRA TIME** Players from almost 100 countries have played in the Premier League since in began in 1992-93. Among the overseas countries best represented are France, Spain, Italy, Holland, Sweden, Norway and Portugal.

SHOOT ANNUAL 2014  45

# A FEW WORDS FROM...

## LEON OSMAN
### EVERTON AND ENGLAND

## IT'S TRUE

Osman scored his first Everton goal three minutes into his first start, against Wolves in 2004.

**YOU WERE A LATE-COMER INTO THE ENGLAND SQUAD AT THE AGE OF 31. CAN YOU STAY THERE?**

"It is important to me that we stay near the top of the league. It wasn't until we started playing the football that we have that I managed to push into the squad. I still feel like I am young in the head and most people at Everton would tell you that."

**WHAT DID THE INTERNATIONAL CALL-UP MEAN TO YOU?**

"To be in the squad means the world to me. I just need to keep my head down, keep working hard and if another chance comes, I have got to take it. As you start to get 30-plus the chances start to diminish but as an English lad you still keep going for your club and if it ever happens that is great."

**HOW DID YOU HEAR ABOUT THE CALL-UP FROM ENGLAND BOSS ROY HODGSON?**

"The manager got the lads together as the training session was coming to an end – there seemed to be a lot more staff around the edge of the pitch than usual. He said that I was in the squad. I knew about the international being the following week but I wasn't expecting to be called up."

**WHAT DID YOUR FAMILY THINK?**

"It was a great moment. My elder son had been out on a school trip. When he came back, I sat him down and put Sky Sports News on for him, with a confused look on his face. I said, 'That's your name, you know.' When he realised he was made up."

**TELL US ABOUT YOUR DEVELOPMENT...**

"I came into first-team football late. I made my debut at 21, became a first team regular at 23, getting into my first England squad at 31. My development always seems to have been late!"

**YOU COMPLETED A DECADE AT THE CLUB IN 2012-13. WHAT WAS THAT LIKE?**

"I've got some great memories from the ten years but we haven't won anything and I would love to do that. You don't just win a cup because you deserve it. It is up to us as players, managers and staff to try and turn what is deserved into actually doing something.

## FACT FILE
**LEON OSMAN**

**Position:** Midfielder
**Birth date:** May 17, 1981
**Birth place:** Wigan
**Height:** 1.73m (5ft 8in)
**Clubs:** Everton, Carlisle United (loan), Derby County (loan)
**International:** England

**DID YOU KNOW?** Osman agreed a new deal at the end of 2012-13 which will keep him at Goodison Park until 2015. Despite the exit of boss David Moyes, who gave the player his debut in 2003, the midfielder now looks set to become a one-club player.

**EXTRA TIME** Osman came through Everton's Academy but when he suffered a broken leg in 2001, that kept him out of action for a year, there were fears about his future as a professional. He's now played more than 370 games.

## SOUTHAMPTON
# RICKIE LAMBERT

### WHAT WAS IT LIKE TO MAKE YOUR PREMIER LEAGUE DEBUT?

"I'd always dreamed of scoring in the Premier League and always believed I had the ability to play at this level. I don't want to play in any other division now. The pace and touch of the players was a big eye-opener for me and it was a big step up. To be actually involved in any game in the Premier League is an honour, especially for Southampton."

### DID YOU SET YOURSELF A TARGET?

"I am enjoying every moment but I haven't set any goal targets. I just want to go out and contribute as much as I can to the team, not just score goals. I'm not about goal tallies and I never have been. I'm about playing to help my team and I feel like I could have helped them with a few more goals across the course of the season."

### WHAT'S THE TOUGHEST PART?

"Losing games and points hurts. I don't feel the pressure but my job is to score goals. I am not happy when I don't score in any game."

### BUT YOU WERE THE JOINT-TOP SCORING ENGLISHMAN IN 2012-13, WITH FRANK LAMPARD WITH 15 GOALS!

"It does sound good and I think when I look back at it this will be a good achievement. For the season I had, I would have thought I could have scored more and I'd liked to have scored more. I would like more and hopefully next year can improve."

### TELL US ABOUT THE 3-1 HOME WIN OVER LIVERPOOL...

"I grew up as a Liverpool fan and all my family are Reds. I'm obviously now a Saints fan. It was a massive game and my family were there, but I am professional and my main focus was to try and get the points. I am just over the moon that my goal helped get all three points."

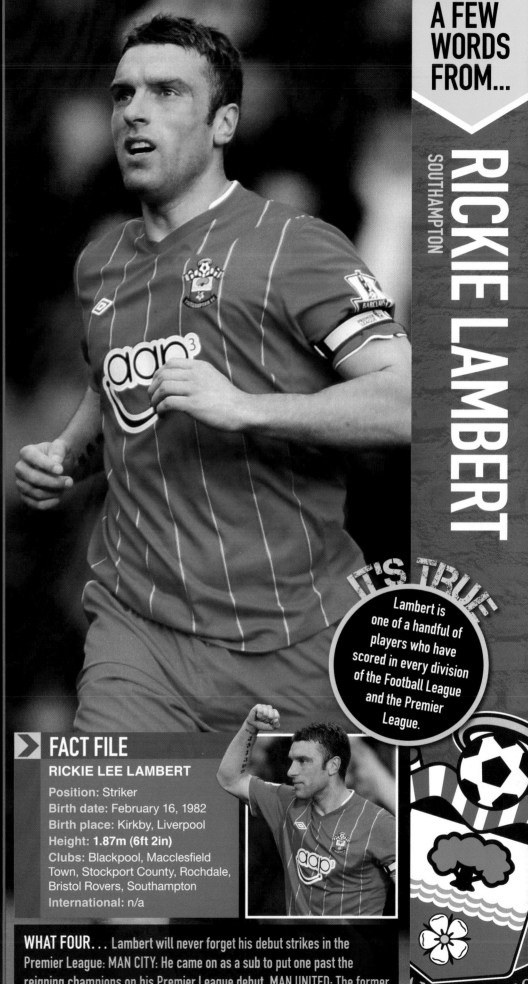

### IT'S TRUE
Lambert is one of a handful of players who have scored in every division of the Football League and the Premier League.

## ▶ FACT FILE

**RICKIE LEE LAMBERT**

**Position:** Striker
**Birth date:** February 16, 1982
**Birth place:** Kirkby, Liverpool
**Height:** **1.87m (6ft 2in)**
**Clubs:** Blackpool, Macclesfield Town, Stockport County, Rochdale, Bristol Rovers, Southampton
**International:** n/a

**WHAT FOUR...** Lambert will never forget his debut strikes in the Premier League: **MAN CITY:** He came on as a sub to put one past the reigning champions on his Premier League debut. **MAN UNITED:** The former title-holders were next to be hit by a Lambert goal. **ASTON VILLA:** His first Premier double in Saints first victory on their return to the top-flight.

EXTRA TIME — Lambert joined Saints from Bristol Rovers in August 2009 for just over £1m. He was manager Alan Pardew's first signing. He scored 36 goals that season, 31 in League One, which made him the top English scorer in all divisions.

SHOOT ANNUAL 2014    47

# THE CRAZY WORLD OF FOOTBALL

CRASH

DIVING FOOTBALLERS WHO WRITHE AROUND THE FLOOR IN PAIN COULD WELL BE FAKING THEIR INJURIES - PLAYERS CAN STAND MORE PAIN THAN ANY OTHER SPORTS PEOPLE! UNIVERSITY RESEARCHERS IN GERMANY RECKON THAT THEIR REGULAR TRAINING AND EXERCISES MAKES THEM TOUGHER.

FORMER MANCHESTER CITY OWNER THAKSIN SHINAWATRA HAD MAGIC CRYSTALS AND PORCELAIN ELEPHANTS BURIED UNDER THE CLUB'S PITCH. THE LUCKY CHARMS WERE MEANT TO ENERGISE THE PLAYERS AND CREATE TEAM HARMONY. BUT THEY NEVER BROUGHT THE CLUB ANY SUCCESS! AFTER THE ITEMS WERE DUG UP CITY WON THE FA CUP AND PREMIER LEAGUE!

HUH?!

POOOW

**TRUE TALES**
• A Chinese football fan died of exhaustion after staying up for ELEVEN days to watch all of Euro 2012.
• A football kicked into the sea in Wicklow, Republic of Ireland, was found 200 miles away in Cornwall.

**BAM**

A FOOTBALL FAN WAS ALL SET TO WIN £500,000 – UNTIL THE REFEREE BLEW HIS WHISTLE!

THE SUPPORTER HAD MADE A SERIES OF 20p BETS WITH BOOKIES ON FOUR DIFFERENT GAMES. HIS FIRST THREE RESULTS CAME IN AS HE HAD PREDICTED. BUT THE REFEREE AT THE LEEDS UNITED v TOTTENHAM FA CUP TIE BLEW HIS WHISTLE JUST BEFORE THE YORKSHIRE SIDE SAW THE BALL HIT THE BACK OF THE NET.

IF THAT "GOAL" HAD STOOD THE FAN WOULD HAVE WON HALF A MILLION POUNDS!

GARETH ROBERTS FOUND HIS SHOOTING BOOTS THANKS TO A HAIRDRYER! WHILST PLAYING FOR DONCASTER HE FOUND HIS BOOTS WERE ROCK HARD, SO THE KITMAN SOAKED THEM IN WATER AND THEN DRIED THEM WITH A HAIRDRYER. ROBERTS THEN SCORED THE WINNER AGAINST WATFORD!

**BIFF**

A FOOTBALL MATCH HAD TO BE ABANDONED BECAUSE OF A FIGHT BETWEEN TWO CHURCH SIDES! THE UNHOLY BRAWL WAS BETWEEN COMMON GROUND UNITED AND ZION ATHLETIC IN THE WEST MIDLANDS AND A PLAYER WHO HAD BEEN SENT-OFF EARLIER EVEN JOINED IN!

ARCHIE THOMPSON EARNED HIMSELF A PLACE IN THE GUINNESS BOOK OF RECORDS BY SCORING 13 GOALS IN A WORLD CUP QUALIFIER. THERE WAS NO SCORE IN THE GAME BETWEEN AUSTRALIA AND AMERICAN SAMOA AFTER TEN MINUTES    BUT THE GAME ENDED 31-0 TO THE AUSSIES. IT WAS APRIL 11, 2001, AS THE SIDES BATTLED TO TRY AND GET TO THE FINALS THE FOLLOWING YEAR. THOMPSON RECKONED EVEN HIS GRANNY COULD HAVE SCORED A HAT-TRICK IN THE GAME. HE WAS SO SURPRISED BY HIS FEAT HE FORGOT TO COLLECT THE MATCH BALL.

**FWOW**

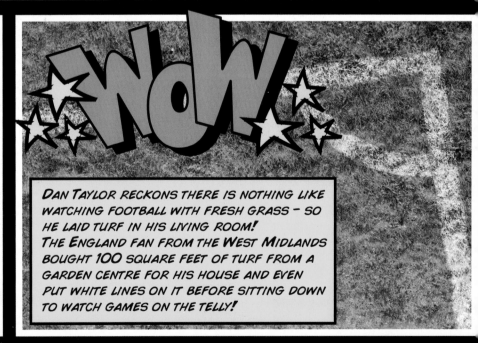

DAN TAYLOR RECKONS THERE IS NOTHING LIKE WATCHING FOOTBALL WITH FRESH GRASS – SO HE LAID TURF IN HIS LIVING ROOM! THE ENGLAND FAN FROM THE WEST MIDLANDS BOUGHT 100 SQUARE FEET OF TURF FROM A GARDEN CENTRE FOR HIS HOUSE AND EVEN PUT WHITE LINES ON IT BEFORE SITTING DOWN TO WATCH GAMES ON THE TELLY!

**PETER CROUCH**

KIT PICTURED:

END OF SEASON 2012-13:

**ANDY CARROLL**

KIT PICTURED:

END OF SEASON 2012-13:

**KEVIN PHILLIPS**

KIT PICTURED:

END OF SEASON 2012-13:

**JACK WILSHERE**

KIT PICTURED:

END OF SEASON 2012-13:

# WHERE AM I?

There are so many transfers and loans in football it's sometimes difficult to remember which player is playing for which team. Can you help out these stars who have got a bit confused... We want you to tell us which team they were playing for in the pictures – and which sides they finished with in season 2012-13. Tip: they may not have played in the pictured kits for some time...

**DAVID BENTLEY**

KIT PICTURED:

END OF SEASON 2012-13:

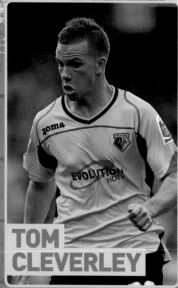

**TOM CLEVERLEY**

KIT PICTURED:

END OF SEASON 2012-13:

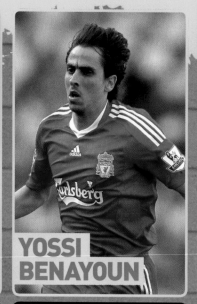

**YOSSI BENAYOUN**

KIT PICTURED:

END OF SEASON 2012-13:

**JERMAINE JENAS**

KIT PICTURED:

END OF SEASON 2012-13:

**EXTRA TIME** Premier League clubs spent a total of £120m on players during the January 2013 transfer window – that was double what the 20 teams forked out the previous year. Watch after Christmas to see what they spend in 2014!

# YOUR GUIDE TO THE CLUBS

BARCLAYS PREMIER LEAGUE

## FACTS ABOUT ALL 20 ENGLISH PREMIER LEAGUE SIDES

PLUS STAR PLAYERS, SCORERS, STATS AND DETAILS FROM SEASON 2012-13

## ARSENAL 4TH

TOP SCORER: Theo Walcott, 21

PLAYER OF THE SEASON: Santi Cazorla

BEST CROWD: 60,112

BEST RESULT: Arsenal 5-2 Tottenham

MEMORABLE MOMENT: Clinching the final Champions League spot on the last day of the season ahead of rivals Tottenham Hotspur. The Gunners won eight and drew two of their last ten matches.

## ASTON VILLA 15TH

TOP SCORER: Christian Benteke, 23

PLAYER OF THE SEASON: Brad Guzan

BEST CROWD: 36,736

BEST RESULT: Villa 6-1 Sunderland

MEMORABLE MOMENT: Securing safety after a tough season in which Villa looked doomed at times. Thrashing Sunderland in April played a big part in upholding the club's ever-present Premier League status.

## CARDIFF CITY
### CHAMPIONSHIP WINNERS

TOP SCORER: Heidar Helguson, 9

PLAYER OF THE SEASON: Mark Hudson

BEST CROWD: 26,588

BEST RESULT: Cardiff 3-0 Forest

MEMORABLE MOMENT: The 0-0 draw at home to Charlton sparked scenes of celebration as Malky Mackay's men secured promotion for the first time.

## CHELSEA 3RD

TOP SCORER: Fernando Torres, 23

PLAYER OF THE SEASON: Juan Mata

BEST CROWD: 41,794

BEST RESULT: Man United 0-1 Chelsea

MEMORABLE MOMENT: Aside from winning the Europa League, the 8-0 thrashing of Villa was overshadowed by a vital 1-0 win at Old Trafford. The victory all but secured the Blues a top-four place.

## CRYSTAL PALACE
### PLAY-OFF WINNERS

TOP SCORER: Glen Murray, 31

PLAYER OF THE SEASON: Mile Jedinak

BEST CROWD: 22,154

BEST RESULT: Palace 1-0 Watford

MEMORABLE MOMENT: Beating rivals Brighton in the play-off semi-final was special but edging out Watford at Wembley to return to the Premier League was the dream day.

## EVERTON 6TH

TOP SCORER: Marouane Fellaini, 12

PLAYER OF THE SEASON: Leighton Baines

BEST CROWD: 39,613

BEST RESULT: Everton 1-0 Man United

MEMORABLE MOMENT: Starting the season with an impressive victory over the eventual champions, then saying goodbye to boss David Moyes before finishing above Liverpool again.

## FULHAM 12TH

TOP SCORER: Dimitar Berbatov, 15

PLAYER OF THE SEASON: Dimitar Berbatov

BEST CROWD: 25,700

BEST RESULT: Tottenham 0-1 Fulham

MEMORABLE MOMENT: A victory at Tottenham and a draw at Arsenal will stick in fans' minds. Dimitar Berbatov, who scored in both matches, added some much-needed class up top.

## HULL CITY
### CHAMPIONSHIP RUNNER-UP

TOP SCORER: Robert Koren, 9

PLAYER OF THE SEASON: Robert Koren

BEST CROWD: 23,812

BEST RESULT: Watford 1-2 Hull City

MEMORABLE MOMENT: Securing promotion with a draw against Cardiff City but that just highlighted how important the win at Watford, who finished third, was earlier in the season.

## LIVERPOOL 7TH

TOP SCORER: Luis Suarez, 30

PLAYER OF THE SEASON: Luis Suarez

BEST CROWD: 45,009

BEST RESULT: Newcastle 0-6 Liverpool

MEMORABLE MOMENT: The win over Tottenham in March was impressive but not as much as the thrashing of Newcastle. The Reds hit the Toon for six at St. James' Park without star man Luis Suarez.

## MANCHESTER CITY 2ND

TOP SCORERS: Sergio Aguero and Carlos Tevez, both 17

PLAYER OF THE SEASON: Pablo Zabaleta

BEST CROWD: 47,386

BEST RESULT: Man United 1-2 Man City

MEMORABLE MOMENT: The win at Old Trafford was a bright spot in what was otherwise a disappointing and trophy-less campaign that resulted in manager Roberto Mancini being sacked.

EXTRA TIME Eleven Premier League managers were either sacked, resigned, retired or their contracts ran out during 2012-13. Chelsea's Robert Di Matteo was the first to be axed on November 21, 2012.

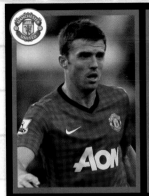

## MANCHESTER UNITED — 1ST

**TOP SCORER:** Robin van Persie, 30

**PLAYER OF THE SEASON:**
Michael Carrick

**BEST CROWD:** 75,605

**BEST RESULT:** Man City 2-3 Man United

**MEMORABLE MOMENT:** Collecting a 20th title and saying goodbye to Sir Alex Ferguson, who retired after 26 years in charge. The win at rivals City was a pivotal moment in the campaign.

## NEWCASTLE UNITED — 16TH

**TOP SCORER:** Papiss Cisse, 13

**PLAYER OF THE SEASON:**
Fabricio Coloccini

**BEST CROWD:** 52,385

**BEST RESULT:** Newcastle 3-2 Chelsea

**MEMORABLE MOMENT:** Securing Premier League survival with a win at QPR after a long and difficult season. Alan Pardew's side disappointed having finished fifth at the end of the previous campaign.

## NORWICH CITY — 11TH

**TOP SCORER:** Grant Holt, 8

**PLAYER OF THE SEASON:**
Sebastien Bassong

**BEST CROWD:** 26,842

**BEST RESULT:** Norwich 1-0 Man United

**MEMORABLE MOMENT:** Beating Manchester United and Arsenal at home and Manchester City away. The thrashing of West Brom was also huge as it secured Norwich's top-flight status.

## SOUTHAMPTON — 14TH

**TOP SCORER:** Rickie Lambert, 15

**FANS' PLAYER OF THE SEASON:**
Morgan Schneiderlin

**BEST CROWD:** 32,070

**BEST RESULT:** Saints 3-1 Man City

**MEMORABLE MOMENT:** Saints ran all the big sides close and beat Liverpool, Chelsea and Manchester City at home, as the team survived a dramatic management switch to survive.

## STOKE CITY — 13TH

**TOP SCORER:** Jon Walters, 11

**PLAYER OF THE SEASON:**
Asmir Begovic

**BEST CROWD:** 27,544

**BEST RESULT:** QPR 0-2 Stoke

**MEMORABLE MOMENT:** The win at strugglers QPR was a huge result, and one that kept Stoke above water. The Potters had previously failed to win in seven and were dangerously close to the drop.

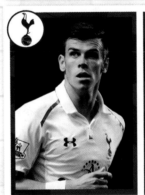

## SUNDERLAND — 17TH

**TOP SCORER:** Steven Fletcher, 11

**PLAYER OF THE SEASON:**
Simon Mignolet

**BEST CROWD:** 47,456

**BEST RESULT:** Newcastle 0-3 Sunderland

**MEMORABLE MOMENT:** Beating your fierce rivals 3-0 in their own backyard doesn't get any better. The win at Newcastle helped keep the Black Cats in the division at the end of campaign.

## SWANSEA CITY — 9TH

**TOP SCORER:** Michu, 22

**PLAYER OF THE SEASON:**
Michu

**BEST CROWD:** 20,650

**BEST RESULT:** Chelsea 0-2 Swansea
(League Cup)

**MEMORABLE MOMENT:** Beating Bradford City 5-0 at Wembley to secure their first-ever major trophy. The victory at Arsenal and Michu's goals were also plus points.

## TOTTENHAM — 5TH

**TOP SCORER:** Gareth Bale, 26

**PLAYER OF THE SEASON:**
Gareth Bale

**BEST CROWD:** 36,736

**BEST RESULT:** Man United 2-3 Tottenham

**MEMORABLE MOMENT:** Beating the champions at Old Trafford was up there with wins over Manchester City, Arsenal and Inter Milan. A host of Bale crackers will also stay in the memory.

## WEST BROM — 8TH

**TOP SCORER:** Romelu Lukaku, 17

**PLAYER OF THE SEASON:**
Gareth McAuley

**BEST CROWD:** 26,438

**BEST RESULT:** Liverpool 0-2 West Brom

**MEMORABLE MOMENT:** Beating Liverpool twice and Chelsea were highlights but the 5-5 draw at the Hawthorns against Man United in Sir Alex Ferguson's last match will live long in the memory.

## WEST HAM — 10TH

**TOP SCORER:** Kevin Nolan, 10

**PLAYER OF THE SEASON:**
Winston Reid

**BEST CROWD:** 35,005

**BEST RESULT:** West Ham 3-1 Chelsea

**MEMORABLE MOMENT:** A second half comeback to defeat rivals Chelsea. The victory ended a run of just once win in six and helped the Hammers' push for survival.

---

**EXTRA TIME** Cardiff City's promotion means they become the second Welsh side to play in the Premier League after Swansea City. The Bluebirds were last in England's top-flight in 1961-62 when the league was still known as the First Division.

# TOP FLIGHT
## STATS, FACTS & TRIVIA YOU NEED TO KNOW!

## PREMIER LEAGUE 2012-13

Arsenal qualified for the Champions League for a 16th consecutive season under Arsene Wenger

Chelsea's Roberto Di Matteo was the first manager to be sacked

Van Persie collected his second consecutive Golden Boot and has scored 56 Premier League goals in the past two seasons

QPR became the first team to go 16 games into a Premier League season without registering a win

Robin van Persie scored in both games against his old club Arsenal

Everton finished in the top seven in nine of 11 seasons under David Moyes

Spurs' Gareth Bale became only the third player to win both the PFA Player and Young Player of the Year Awards.

## HIGHEST TOTAL HOME ATTENDANCES

|  |  |
|------|-----------|
| Man United | 1,435,063 |
| Arsenal | 1,141,507 |
| Newcastle | 959,826 |
| Man City | 845,452 |
| Liverpool | 805,432 |
| Sunderland | 770,344 |
| Chelsea | 745,992 |
| Everton | 690,763 |
| Tottenham | 648,503 |
| Aston Villa | 666,135 |
| West Ham | 659,677 |
| Southampton | 555,063 |
| Stoke City | 511,467 |
| Norwich | 506,762 |
| Fulham | 482,492 |
| West Brom | 455,400 |
| Reading | 453,378 |
| Swansea | 366,672 |
| Wigan | 345,126 |
| QPR | 337,808 |

**EXTRA TIME** Champions Manchester United collected £60.8m in television broadcast fees during 2012-13, the highest amount ever received in the Premier League. Bottom side Wigan were handed £40.7m

## BAD GUYS

**Most disciplinary points**
Craig Gardner (Sunderland) 12
**Most reds**
Steve Sidwell (Fulham) 2
Steven Pienaar (Everton) 2

Manchester United scored the most goals (86) and QPR the least (30)

Manchester City's Joe Hart won the Golden Glove for most Premier League clean sheets for a third straight year. The England stopper didn't concede a goal in 18 games – one better than the previous season

Manchester City conceded the least (34) and Reading and Wigan the most (73)

1,063 goals were scored throughout the campaign

Christian Benteke's 19 league goals means he has hit the most Premier League goals in a season for the Aston Villa

There were 51 own-goals – Southampton's Jos Hooiveld hit three!

There were 86 penalties in the 2012-13 season – 18 were missed

Chelsea's 8-0 win over Aston Villa matched their 8-0 victory against Wigan in 2010 to equal their biggest-ever win in the Premier League

QPR had the oldest average aged squad (28) and Liverpool the youngest (23.22)

## TOP SCORERS

Robin van Persie (Man United) 26
Luis Suarez (Liverpool) 23
Gareth Bale (Tottenham) 21
Christian Benteke (Aston Villa) 19
Michu (Swansea City) 18

## MOST ASSISTS

Juan Mata (Chelsea) 12
Santi Cazorla (Arsenal) 11
Eden Hazard (Chelsea) 11
Wayne Rooney (Man United) 10
Theo Walcott (Arsenal) 10

Stoke City picked up the most yellow cards (11)

Arsenal collected the most red cards (5)

The 5-5 draw between West Brom and Manchester United was the first time Sir Alex Ferguson, who was in charge of his 1,500th and final game, had overseen a match with that scoreline

**EXTRA TIME** Wigan Athletic, relegated after eight years in the top-flight, became the first club to win the FA Cup and be relegated from the Premier League in the same season.

SHOOT ANNUAL 2014 55

# RED REVENGE!

## UNITED TAKE THE TITLE BACK FROM CITY

After losing the title to their rivals in the final seconds of the 2011-12 Premier League season, Manchester United were more determined than ever to regain their crown.

Boss Sir Alex Ferguson showed his intent by capturing Arsenal striker Robin van Persie for £24m in summer 2012.

And the Dutchman ended up being the difference between United and Manchester City in more ways than one.

RVP scored a last-minute winner in the Red Devils' 3-2 victory at the Sky Blues in December, and his Golden Boot-winning 26 goals during 2012-13 played a huge part in United claiming their 20th league title.

Premier League victory was wrapped up by April 22, as Fergie's men defeated Aston Villa 3-0 at Old Trafford, thanks to a Van Persie hat-trick.

United ended up 11 points ahead of City, whose trophy-less campaign cost manager Roberto Mancini his job, exactly 12 months after he had guided the club to their first top-flight title in 44 years.

Ferguson shocked the football world two weeks later by announcing his retirement at the end of the season after 26-years in the United job and 13 Premier League title victories.

The Red Devils celebrated his last two games in charge with a Rio Ferdinand strike sealing a late 2-1 win against Swansea at Old Trafford followed by a thrilling 5-5 draw at West Brom.

Another Scot, Everton boss David Moyes, has replaced Fergie in the United dugout.

Arsenal grabbed the final Champions League spot, finishing a point above North London rivals Spurs.

Southampton and West Ham United both enjoyed decent returns to the Premier League, finishing 14th and 10th respectively.

However, Reading, who sacked manager Brian McDermott in March, were relegated after just one season, with former Southampton boss Nigel Adkins in charge.

Wigan, who lifted their first major trophy by winning the FA Cup, also went down after eight seasons in the top-flight.

QPR finished rock bottom following a disastrous season of big money signings, a management sacking and many off-field controversies.

## UNITED'S TITLE STARS

**TOP SCORER:** *Robin van Persie, 26*
**MOST ASSISTS:** *Wayne Rooney 10*
**BAD BOY:** *Rafael, 1 red card*

## WHAT THE BOSS SAID...

"They focused on the challenge of City and came up trumps. Our consistency for the last 20 years is unbelievable. This club never gives in. From Sir Matt Busby, the Munich Disaster, to rebuilding and to win the European Cup, that tells you the history of United. Every player who comes to this club has to have that engrained. We have lived up to the expectation"
*Sir Alex Ferguson*

## WHAT THE PLAYERS SAID...

"It's always sweet when you win the title and it's nice to do it in the right way and in style, not on goal difference. We have won it outright and we have won it comfortably." *Rio Ferdinand*

"This team is unbelievable. Every team of champions starts with a good atmosphere and the idea that every single person wants to share success and everybody wants to play their part in it. That is how you achieve big things and win trophies." *Robin van Persie*

"Some of the performances have been superb. Whenever you win the Premier League it is something special. Obviously, if you look at the end of last season that was a huge disappointment. To come back the following year and perform so strongly means it must rank really high." *Ryan Giggs*

## FINAL TABLE 2012-13

|    | Team | PL | GD | PTS |
|----|------|----|----|----|
| 01 | Man United | 38 | 43 | 89 |
| 02 | Man City | 38 | 32 | 78 |
| 03 | Chelsea | 38 | 36 | 75 |
| 04 | Arsenal | 38 | 35 | 73 |
| 05 | Tottenham | 38 | 20 | 72 |
| 06 | Everton | 38 | 15 | 63 |
| 07 | Liverpool | 38 | 28 | 61 |
| 08 | West Brom | 38 | -4 | 49 |
| 09 | Swansea | 38 | -4 | 46 |
| 10 | West Ham | 38 | -8 | 46 |
| 11 | Norwich | 38 | -17 | 44 |
| 12 | Fulham | 38 | -10 | 43 |
| 13 | Stoke | 38 | -11 | 42 |
| 14 | Southampton | 38 | -11 | 41 |
| 15 | Aston Villa | 38 | -22 | 41 |
| 16 | Newcastle | 38 | -23 | 41 |
| 17 | Sunderland | 38 | -13 | 39 |
| 18 | Wigan | 38 | -26 | 36 |
| 19 | Reading | 38 | -30 | 28 |
| 20 | QPR | 38 | -30 | 25 |

# CHAMPIONSHIP
# WELSH WIZARDS

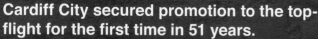

**Cardiff City secured promotion to the top-flight for the first time in 51 years.**

Malky Mackay's side topped the table from late November and won 25 of their 46 games throughout the 2012-13 campaign.

The Welsh side were controversially rebranded prior to the start of the campaign, when their traditional blue home strip was changed to red by their Malaysian owners.

However, the fans were quickly back onside as the Bluebirds claimed the promotion that they had come close to on a number of occasions in recent years following a 0-0 draw against Charlton Athletic.

Hull City are also back in the Premier League after a dramatic final day. After failing to win in three, Steve Bruce's men needed to match Watford's result to clinch second spot.

The Tigers missed a penalty and then conceded to a last-minute spot-kick against Cardiff, but Watford's defeat to Leeds meant Hull returned to the top-flight for the first time since 2010.

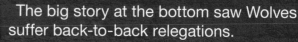

The big story at the bottom saw Wolves suffer back-to-back relegations.

Boss Dean Saunders couldn't save the Molineux club from dropping into the third tier for the first time in 24 years.

Peterborough United also went down despite collecting 54 points – four more than the previous season.

Bristol City's fate was sealed midway through April after a season to forget.

# CHAMPIONSHIP
# PLAY-OFF FINAL

Crystal Palace returned to the Premier League for the first time since suffering relegation in 2005 after defeating Watford 1-0 at Wembley.

A magnificent penalty from veteran striker Kevin Phillips in extra time secured the Eagles a deserved victory.

The South London side looked by far the most dangerous throughout, with Wilfried Zaha tormenting the Hornets' backline.

And it was the England international who won the vital spot-kick as he was taken down by Marco Cassetti.

Substitute Phillips made no mistake from 12 yards, smashing the ball into the top corner.

Manager Ian Holloway, who lost out in the previous year's final as manager of Blackpool, said: "I am so proud of these players. I am so proud of the club. We are in the Premier League so, God help us."

## CHAMPIONSHIP FINAL TABLE

|  | | PL | GD | PTS |
|---|---|---|---|---|
| 01 | Cardiff City | 46 | 27 | 87 |
| 02 | Hull City | 46 | 9 | 79 |
| 03 | Watford | 46 | 27 | 77 |
| 04 | Brighton | 46 | 26 | 75 |
| 05 | Crystal Palace | 46 | 11 | 72 |
| 06 | Leicester City | 46 | 23 | 68 |
| 07 | Bolton wanderers | 46 | 8 | 68 |
| 08 | Nottingham Forest | 46 | 4 | 67 |
| 09 | Charlton Athletic | 46 | 6 | 65 |
| 10 | Derby County | 46 | 3 | 61 |
| 11 | Burnley | 46 | 2 | 61 |
| 12 | Birmingham City | 46 | -6 | 61 |
| 13 | Leeds United | 46 | -9 | 61 |
| 14 | Ipswich Town | 46 | -13 | 60 |
| 15 | Blackpool | 46 | -1 | 59 |
| 16 | Middlesbrough | 46 | -9 | 59 |
| 17 | Blackburn Rovers | 46 | -7 | 58 |
| 18 | Sheffield Wednesday | 46 | -8 | 58 |
| 19 | Huddersfield Town | 46 | -20 | 58 |
| 20 | Millwall | 46 | -11 | 56 |
| 21 | Barnsley | 46 | -14 | 55 |
| 22 | Peterborough | 46 | -9 | 54 |
| 23 | Wolves | 46 | -14 | 51 |
| 24 | Bristol City | 46 | -25 | 41 |

## 2012-13 STATS

**TOP SCORERS**
| | | |
|---|---|---|
| Glenn Murray *(Crystal Palace)* | 30 |
| Jordan Rhodes *(Blackburn)* | 29 |
| Charlie Austin *(Burnley)* | 25 |
| Matej Vydra *(Watford)* | 22 |

**MOST ASSISTS**
| | |
|---|---|
| Tom Ince *(Blackpool)* | 14 |
| Robbie Brady *(Hull City)* | 13 |

**BAD BOYS**
Most disciplinary points:
| | |
|---|---|
| Shane Lowry *(Millwall)* | 15 |
| Daniel Pudil *(Watford)* | 13 |
| Dean Marney *(Burnley)* | 13 |
| Marco Cassetti *(Watford)* | 13 |

**HIGHEST AVERAGE ATTENDANCE:** Brighton 26,236

# LEAGUE ONE
# DONNY DELIGHT

Doncaster Rovers snatched the League One title in the final seconds, on the final day of the season.

Brian Flynn's men would've had to settle for a play-off spot had Brentford's Marcello Trotta converted a last gasp penalty in injury time.

But his miss resulted in James Coppinger finishing a counter attack at Griffin Park and sealing the title for Donny.

Relegated from the Championship in 2012, Rovers bounced back at the first attempt.

Bournemouth, who won 22 of 35 matches under returning boss Eddie Howe, finished second, one point behind the Yorkshire side.

It's only the second time the Cherries have been promoted to the second tier, a great achievement for a club that nearly went out of business in 2008.

Portsmouth were relegated to the fourth tier just three years after dropping out the Premier League.

Scunthorpe, Hartlepool and Bury joined them in League Two for 2013-14.

## LEAGUE ONE FINAL TABLE

|     |                   | PL | GD  | PTS |
|-----|-------------------|----|-----|-----|
| 01  | Doncaster Rovers  | 46 | 18  | 84  |
| 02  | Bournemouth       | 46 | 23  | 83  |
| 03  | Brentford         | 46 | 15  | 79  |
| 04  | Yeovil Town       | 46 | 15  | 77  |
| 05  | Sheffield United  | 46 | 14  | 75  |
| 06  | Swindon Town      | 46 | 33  | 74  |
| 07  | Leyton Orient     | 46 | 7   | 71  |
| 08  | MK Dons           | 46 | 17  | 70  |
| 09  | Walsall           | 46 | 7   | 68  |
| 10  | Crawley Town      | 46 | 1   | 68  |
| 11  | Tranmere Rovers   | 46 | 10  | 67  |
| 12  | Notts County      | 46 | 12  | 65  |
| 13  | Crewe Alexandra   | 46 | -8  | 65  |
| 14  | Preston North End | 46 | 5   | 59  |
| 15  | Coventry City     | 46 | 7   | 55  |
| 16  | Shrewsbury        | 46 | -6  | 55  |
| 17  | Carlisle United   | 46 | -12 | 55  |
| 18  | Stevenage         | 46 | -17 | 54  |
| 19  | Oldham Athletic   | 46 | -13 | 51  |
| 20  | Colchester United | 46 | -21 | 51  |
| 21  | Scunthorpe        | 46 | -24 | 48  |
| 22  | Bury              | 46 | -28 | 41  |
| 23  | Hartlepool        | 46 | -28 | 41  |
| 24  | Portsmouth        | 46 | -32 | 32  |

## 2012-13 STATS

### TOP SCORERS
| | |
|---|---|
| Paddy Madden (Yeovil) | 24 |
| Clayton Donaldson (Brentford) | 20 |
| Leon Clarke (Coventry) | 19 |
| Will Grigg (Walsall) | 19 |
| Brett Pitman (Bournemouth) | 19 |

### MOST ASSISTS
| | |
|---|---|
| David Cotterill (Doncaster) | 20 |
| Mark Duffy (Scunthorpe) | 15 |

### BAD BOYS
Most disciplinary points:
| | |
|---|---|
| Harry Arter (Bournemouth) | 14 |
| Harry Maguire (Sheffield United) | 13 |

### HIGHEST AVERAGE ATTENDANCE
Sheffield United 18,472

# LEAGUE ONE
# PLAY-OFF FINAL

Yeovil were promoted to the second tier for the first time in their history after defeating Brentford 2-1 at Wembley.

Top scorer Paddy Madden and Daniel Burn gave the Glovers a 2-0 first half lead. Harlee Dean pulled one back for the Bees but Gary Johnson's men held on.

# LEAGUE TWO
# GILLS GLEE

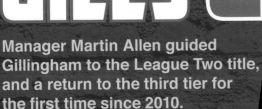

Manager Martin Allen guided Gillingham to the League Two title, and a return to the third tier for the first time since 2010.

The Gills, who topped the division for the majority of the campaign, finally secured promotion after a 1-0 win at home against Torquay.

The Kent side only conceded 39 goals, 20 better than runners-up Rotherham.

The Millers, who moved into their New York Stadium at the start of the campaign, won their final five games to clinch promotion in boss Steve Evans' first full season in charge.

Micky Adams' Port Vale clinched the final automatic spot in a season that saw them occupy a top-three place since September.

Vale striker Tom Pope was the division's top scorer after firing an impressive 31 goals, which included three hat-tricks.

At the bottom, Barnet couldn't survive relegation to the Conference on the final day for a fourth season in a row after losing 2-0 at Northampton.

Aldershot returned to non-league football for the first time since the 2007-08 campaign.

**GILLINGHAM FOOTBALL CLUB**

## LEAGUE TWO FINAL TABLE

| | | PL | GD | PTS |
|---|---|---|---|---|
| 01 | Gillingham | 46 | 27 | 83 |
| 02 | Rotherham | 46 | 15 | 79 |
| 03 | Port Vale | 46 | 35 | 78 |
| 04 | Burton Albion | 46 | 6 | 76 |
| 05 | Cheltenham Town | 46 | 7 | 75 |
| 06 | Northampton | 46 | 9 | 73 |
| 07 | Bradford | 46 | 11 | 69 |
| 08 | Chesterfield | 46 | 15 | 67 |
| 09 | Oxford United | 46 | -1 | 65 |
| 10 | Exeter City | 46 | 1 | 64 |
| 11 | Southend United | 46 | 6 | 61 |
| 12 | Rochdale | 46 | -2 | 61 |
| 13 | Fleetwood | 46 | -2 | 60 |
| 14 | Bristol Rovers | 46 | -9 | 60 |
| 15 | Wycombe Wanderers | 46 | -10 | 60 |
| 16 | Morecambe | 46 | -6 | 58 |
| 17 | York City | 46 | -10 | 55 |
| 18 | Accrington Stanley | 46 | -17 | 54 |
| 19 | Torquay United | 46 | -7 | 53 |
| 20 | Wimbledon | 46 | -22 | 53 |
| 21 | Plymouth Argyle | 46 | -9 | 52 |
| 22 | Dagenham & Redbridge | 46 | -7 | 51 |
| 23 | Barnet | 46 | -12 | 51 |
| 24 | Aldershot | 46 | -18 | 48 |

## 2012-13 STATS

### TOP SCORERS
| | |
|---|---|
| Tom Pope *(Port Vale)* | 31 |
| Nahki Wells *(Bradford)* | 22 |
| Jamie Cureton *(Exeter)* | 21 |
| Daniel Nardiello *(Rotherham)* | 19 |

### MOST ASSISTS
| | |
|---|---|
| Kevan Hurst *(Southend)* | 15 |
| Chris Hackett *(Northampton)* | 14 |

### BAD BOYS
Most disciplinary points:
| | |
|---|---|
| Rene Howe *(Torquay)* | 15 |
| Tom Parkes *(Bristol Rovers)* | 14 |
| Josh Scowen *(Wycombe)* | 14 |
| Clarke Carlisle *(Northampton)* | 14 |

### HIGHEST AVERAGE ATTENDANCE
Bradford City 10,502

# LEAGUE TWO
# PLAY-OFF FINAL

Bradford City made it second time lucky at Wembley, defeating Northampton Town 3-0.

The Bantams had been thrashed 5-0 by Swansea in the League Cup Final but bounced back to make a return to League One. Goals from James Hanson, Rory McArdle and Nahki Wells in the opening 28 minutes sealed victory for Phil Parkinson's side.

# ALL THE WINNERS!

## WHO WON WHAT IN 2012-13

WINNERS
UEFA CHAMPIONS LEAGUE 2012/13

### CHAMPIONS LEAGUE
# BAYERN MUNICH

A late Arjen Robben goal saw Bayern Munich beat rivals Borussia Dortmund 2-1 in the first all-German European Cup final. Mario Mandzukic gave Jupp Heynckes' side the lead on the hour before İlkay Gundogan's spot-kick got Jurgen Klopp's men back on level terms just seven minutes later. But Bayern, who lost out to Chelsea on their own patch in the 2012 final, snatched their fifth European Cup and first since 2001 when Dutchman Robben prodded home with just a minute to go.

### PREMIER LEAGUE CHAMPIONS
# MANCHESTER UNITED

| RUNNERS-UP | CHAMPIONS LEAGUE |
|---|---|
| MANCHESTER CITY | CHELSEA |
| | ARSENAL |

RELEGATED
QPR, READING, WIGAN

**EXTRA TIME** Bayern Munich's fifth European Cup win puts them level on victories with Liverpool. AC Milan have won the competition seven times but the most victories so far is nine by Real Madrid.

## CHAMPIONSHIP CHAMPIONS

### CARDIFF CITY

| AUTOMATIC PROMOTION | PLAY-OFF FINAL |
|---|---|
| HULL CITY | CRYSTAL PALACE 1 WATFORD 0 |

**RELEGATED**
PETERBOROUGH, WOLVES, BRISTOL CITY

## LEAGUE ONE CHAMPIONS

### DONCASTER ROVERS

| AUTOMATIC PROMOTION | PLAY-OFF FINAL |
|---|---|
| BOURNEMOUTH | YEOVIL TOWN 2 BRENTFORD 1 |

**RELEGATED**
SCUNTHORPE, HARTLEPOOL, PORTSMOUTH, BURY

## LEAGUE TWO CHAMPIONS

### GILLINGHAM

| AUTOMATIC PROMOTION | PLAY-OFF FINAL |
|---|---|
| ROTHERHAM PORT VALE | BRADFORD CITY 3 NORTHAMPTON 0 |

**RELEGATED**
BARNET, ALDERSHOT

## CONFERENCE

### MANSFIELD TOWN

**PLAY-OFF FINAL**
WREXHAM 0-2 NEWPORT COUNTY

## SCOTTISH PREMIER LEAGUE

### CELTIC

Neil Lennon guided his side to a 44th title. The Bhoys finished 16 points clear of runners-up Motherwell.

## SCOTTISH CUP

### CELTIC

Celtic wrapped up a domestic double by beating Hibernian 3-0 at Hampden Park. Gary Hooper's first half brace and Joe Ledley's late drive saw off the spirited Edinburgh outfit.

## SCOTTISH LEAGUE CUP

### ST. MIRREN

A 3-2 victory over Hearts secured the Saints' first major trophy since 1987. Goals from Esmael Goncalves, Steven Thompson and Conor Newton ensured victory.

**EXTRA TIME** Celtic's latest Scottish league title puts them ten behind the 54 that have been lifted by their rivals Rangers.

## LEAGUE CUP
## SWANSEA CITY

The Swans secured their first-ever major trophy with a 5-0 win over League Two side Bradford City. Nathan Dyer and Jonathan De Guzman doubles, and a Michu strike sealed the emphatic, historic victory.

# 2013 WINNE

## FA CUP
## WIGAN ATHLETIC

Wigan lifted their first major trophy by snatching a shock 1-0 win against Manchester City at Wembley. Nobody gave the Latics a chance going into the match, but a 90th minute Ben Watson header secured a deserved victory for Roberto Martinez's side.

## JOHNSTONE'S PAINTS TROPHY
## CREWE ALEXANDRA

A goal in each half from Luke Murphy and Max Clayton saw League One Crewe defeat League Two Southend United in a dominant performance.

**EXTRA TIME** Wigan's FA Cup win rates alongside other major final shocks. Sunderland beat Leeds in 1973; Man United lost to Southampton in 1976; in 1980 West Ham beat Arsenal; and Wimbledon beat Liverpool in 1988. All scores were 1-0.

## PFA PLAYER, YOUNG PLAYER AND FOOTBALL WRITERS' FOOTBALLER OF THE YEAR

### GARETH BALE

The Welshman swept up the individual awards after a superb season. The Spurs winger was the third-highest scorer in the Premier League with 21 goals and scored 26 times in all games for the North London side. He almost won many matches single-handed, with his pace, power, quick feet and stunning accuracy from long range consistently lighting up games.

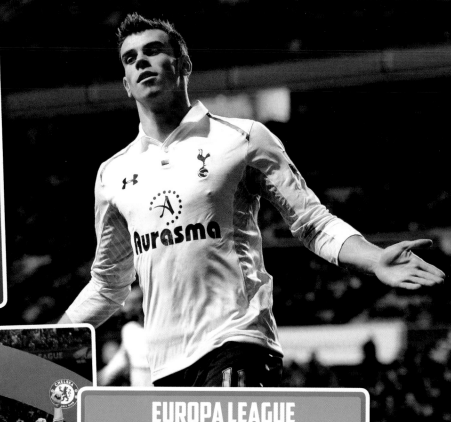

WINNERS UEFA EUROPA LEAGUE 2013

### EUROPA LEAGUE

### CHELSEA

Chelsea won their second European trophy in successive seasons after defeating Benfica 2-1. Oscar Cardoza cancelled out Fernando Torres' opener, before a Branislav Ivanovic injury time header saw the Blues dramatically snatch the trophy.

### FA TROPHY FINAL

#### GRIMSBY 1 - 1 WREXHAM
#### (WREXHAM WON 4-1 ON PENALTIES)

Andy Cook gave Grimsby the lead before Kevin Thornton leveled from the spot. But Wrexham became the first Welsh club to lift the FA Trophy after Johnny Hunt struck the winning penalty in a tense shoot-out.

### FA VASE FINAL

#### SPENNYMOOR TOWN 2
#### TUNBRIDGE WELLS 1

The Northern Football League Division One side saw off the Kent outfit at Wembley. Keith Graydon smashed home the winner with just under ten minutes remaining.

| SPAIN LA LIGA | ITALY SERIE A | FRANCE LIGUE 1 | GERMANY BUNDESLIGA | HOLLAND EREDIVISIE |
|---|---|---|---|---|
| CHAMPIONS BARCELONA | CHAMPIONS JUVENTUS | CHAMPIONS PSG | CHAMPIONS BAYERN MUNICH | CHAMPIONS AJAX |
| RUNNERS-UP REAL MADRID | RUNNERS-UP NAPOLI | RUNNERS-UP MARSEILLE | RUNNERS-UP BORUSSIA DORTMUND | RUNNERS-UP PSV EINDHOVEN |

**EXTRA TIME** Lionel Messi, voted the best player on the planet for the past four years, scored 46 goals in 32 La Liga games as Barcelona lifted the La Liga trophy. It was their 22nd title, won back after losing it in 2011-12 to Real Madrid.

SHOOT ANNUAL 2014 **65**

# FUNNY OLD GAME

**Sometimes football can get a bit too serious. So *Shoot* takes a lighter hearted look at our favourite game...**

Bet you can't throw a ball as well as a dart...

What do you mean, you've never heard of Port Vale!

DARTS ACE PHIL THE POWER TAYLOR DIDN'T THINK MUCH OF RAFAEL VAN DER VAART LEAVING SPURS

PHEWEEEE!

ARSENAL'S THEO WALCOTT RECKONS SOMEONE HAS DROPPED ONE! WE KNOW WHO'S GETTING THE BLAME...

WIND CREATED BY THE ONE-MAN PITCH INVASION FLATTENED THE BAYERN MUNICH PLAYERS

LEWIS HOLTBY HEARD THE PREMIER LEAGUE WAS A BIT DIFFERENT WHEN HE JOINED TOTTENHAM BUT HE DIDN'T EXPECT SUCH UNUSUAL OPPOSITION

AUSSIE KEEPER MARK SCHWARZER GOT THE BIRD AT CRAVEN COTTAGE!

KEEPER PADDY KENNY'S MUM HAD WARNED HIM NOT TO PULL FUNNY FACES.

SOMEONE FORGOT TO TELL STEWART DOWNING AND JAMES MILNER TO REMOVE THE COAT HANGERS BEFORE GETTING DRESSED!

HARRY REDKNAPP FAILED IN HIS AUDITION FOR STRICTLY COME DANCING

BEN FOSTER'S FROG IMPRESSION WASN'T THAT IMPRESSIVE

NO MATTER HOW HARD HE TRIED, GARETH BALE APPEARED TO HAVE A PROBLEM GRABBING A DRINK OF WATER...

This is not so glovely!

BLACKBURN'S JAKE KEANE KNEW HE SHOULDN'T HAVE STUFFED HIS KEEPER GLOVES DOWN HIS PANTS.

Who had the beans or curry?

THE MAN UNITED FAN WAS READY FOR THE PHANTOM FARTER OF OLD TRAFFORD

Where are my ten team-mates?

HE'S SO GOOD THAT BARCELONA DECIDED TO SEND MESSI OUT ON HIS OWN AND GIVE THE OTHER TEAM A CHANCE

TORRES WONDERED IF HE COULD GET TO THE BALL WHILST LAMPARD WASN'T LOOKING.

You're flagging a bit Ashley!

NOW YOU KNOW WHY ASHLEY COLE WAS TALKING IN A RATHER HIGH-PITCHED VOICE!

This is my falling Eagle impression

GLENN MURRAY OF CRYSTAL PALACE WAS JUST SO LAID BACK ABOUT THE GAME!

How do you get 'up the pole'?

RONALDO COULDN'T QUITE GET THE HANG OF IT WHEN HE WAS TOLD TO KEEP THE CORNER LOW...

My you appear to have big furry hands...

FERGIE DIDN'T REALISE THAT HE WAS ABOUT TO BE MASHED BY A MONSTER

# SPOT THE DIFFERENCE!

ARSENAL V SPURS

A

B

Two pictures from two big matches – and our clever designer has made SIX changes to each. Spot the Differences from picture A to picture B in each case and then draw circles around the changes.

## STOKE V READING

# PREMIER LEAGUE
## SECRETS

### CAR PARK...

Defender Patrice Evra bought midfielder Park Ji-Sung a red Ferrari when they both played at Manchester United. But it was only a toy one!

The Frenchman had promised to buy a car after he had been set up for a goal – and it was meant to replace one Park crashed on ice.

## STUFF THAT TOP PLAYERS MIGHT NOT WANT YOU TO KNOW!

### HIGH NOTES

Lanky England striker Peter Crouch reportedly forked out £3,000 for a karaoke machine so that he could try to out-sing some of his footballing mates.

Hope those friends don't include Republic of Ireland striker Shane Long who can not only sing, but also plays the guitar. Check him out on YouTube!

### CAR GONE...

Paul Scholes left his car running – and it disappeared from outside his home!

The former Man United and England midfielder had been de-icing his windscreen when he popped indoors. When he returned the Chevrolet Captiva had been stolen from his drive.

### SKY GAZER

When Phil Neville tells his mates he's been watching sky – he doesn't mean he's been keeping an eye on brother Gary on Sky Sports.

The younger Neville brother is a keen watcher of clouds!

From his posh flat in a Manchester Tower he has watched the "amazing" shapes the clouds make as the weather changes.

Handy in the rain capital of England....

### GAME BOY

David Luiz keeps in touch with his mates overseas by playing *Call of Duty* on line. Chelsea's Brazil defender plays against his international team-mates who are with clubs in Russia, Spain and other European countries.

## THAT'S PONY!

Legendary Arsenal and England keeper David Seaman cut off that ridiculous ponytail back in 2005.

But he's still got it… stuffed in a drawer at his home! He says that rather than auction if off for charity he has hung on to the hair just in case he wants to wear it again. Sell, David, sell…

## ALIEN INVASION!

Chelsea have some new supporters – aliens from outer space! Secret government documents – now made public – reveal that a UFO was spotted over Stamford Bridge when the Blues played Manchester United.

United won the FA Cup sixth round replay 2-0 in March 1999. Now the Red Devils are believed to have fans that really are on another planet…

## EARLY SCORER

Rickie Lambert is famed for his rise from the lower divisions to Premier League status with Southampton.

But the striker actually hit the back of the net at Liverpool when he was just ten-years-old!

He was playing in a local cup final for Kirkby Boys but his side lost 3-2, as he scored at the Anfield Road end.

## CRYING SHAME

Cool, calculated defender Rio Ferdinand is…a crybaby!

The Man United and former England ace admits he blubbed at the sad bits of X Factor and had to keep a supply of tissues handy.

## THAT'S IRISH!

Midfielder James McClean bought himself a flash Lamborghini – even thought he hadn't passed his driving test.

The Republic of Ireland winger was meant to be keeping a low profile at the Stadium of Light.

Don't think he'll do that with such a motor!

**LEARNER DRIVER**

## HE'S THE JUAN!

Juan Mata could have been a pop star if he hadn't turned his back on music to shine on a football pitch.

The Spain and Chelsea midfielder was such a good singer at school that his teacher tried to persuade him not to take up football!

## LEFT, RIGHT…

Some footballers have amazing superstitions – and England's Phil Jones is one of them!

The Man United star has to put his left sock on first for home matches and his right sock is slipped on first at away games!

"I just can't help it and know it is weird," admitted the former Blackburn man.

# GROUND GAME!

You know all about the biggest stadia around, don't you? Prove it with our great ground game! We want you to match the picture to the name of the stadium, which club plays there and try to guess the correct crowd capacity of each ground. The answers are on page 76. No cheating!

## A

GROUND

TEAM

CAPACITY

## B

GROUND

TEAM

CAPACITY

## C

GROUND

TEAM

CAPACITY

## D

GROUND

TEAM

CAPACITY

## E

GROUND

TEAM

CAPACITY

## F

GROUND

TEAM

CAPACITY

| GROUNDS | TEAMS | CAPACITY |
|---|---|---|
| ST. JAMES' PARK | BRIGHTON | 75,800 |
| ANFIELD | MANCHESTER UNITED | 52,300 |
| OLD TRAFFORD | ARSENAL | 30,750 |
| CITY GROUND | NEWCASTLE UNITED | 60,300 |
| EMIRATES STADIUM | NOTTINGHAM FOREST | 45,500 |
| AMEX STADIUM | LIVERPOOL | 30,500 |

**EXTRA TIME** The biggest crowd at a domestic football game in England was the 84,569 at Manchester City Maine Road ground for an FA Cup Sixth Round game against Stoke City in 1934.

# UNITED NATIONS

The English Premier League contains top players from all over the world. *Shoot* has created a multi-national side from 11 different countries but can you place our team members in their correct positions on the pitch? We also want to know where they are from – but have given you a hand by listing their home countries.

|  |  |  |
|---|---|---|
| Goalkeeper: | Player:........................................ | Country:........................ |
| Right back: | Player:........................................ | Country:........................ |
| Central defender: | Player:........................................ | Country:........................ |
| Central defender: | Player:........................................ | Country:........................ |
| Left back: | Player:........................................ | Country:........................ |
| Right wing: | Player:........................................ | Country:........................ |
| Central midfielder: | Player:........................................ | Country:........................ |
| Central midfielder: | Player:........................................ | Country:........................ |
| Left wing: | Player:........................................ | Country:........................ |
| Striker: | Player:........................................ | Country:........................ |
| Striker: | Player:........................................ | Country:........................ |

## PLAYERS

CESAR AZPILICUETA
JUSSI JAASKELAINEN
DAVIDE SANTON
DIMITAR BERBATOV
YOHAN CABAYE
GARETH BALE
YOUSSOUF MULUMBU
VINCENT KOMPANY
DEMBA BA
PHIL JAGIELKA
ANTONIO VALENCIA

## COUNTRIES

ITALY
DR CONGO
SENEGAL
BELGIUM
FINLAND
ENGLAND
SPAIN
FRANCE
BULGARIA
WALES
ECUADOR

# SUPER FRANK

## LAMPARD'S THE GUY WHO LIGHTS UP CHELSEA

If the club thought their supporters were unhappy about the appointment of interim manager Rafa Benitez, Chelsea could have faced a fans' riot if Frank Lampard had been allowed to leave at the end of last season.

Everyone knew that 'Super Frank' wanted to stay and that the supporters didn't want him to go anywhere else, despite reported interest from Manchester United and LA Galaxy.

So when the club's record scorer agreed to sign on for another year at Stamford Bridge there were sighs of relief all round...

### DID YOU EVER THINK YOU WOULD ACTUALLY LEAVE THE BLUES?

"After I was injured for two months at the start of the year I did wonder, but knew it was up to me to get my head down and show I wanted to stay. I didn't come close to anything else, it was always my desire to stay."

### YOU BROKE BOBBY TAMBLING'S GOAL-SCORING RECORD OF 202 GOALS FOR THE CLUB LAST SEASON. WHAT WAS THAT LIKE?

"It means everything, it's amazing. The support I've had from team-mates, I'm thankful to every one of them because they're the ones that put it on a plate for me sometimes. And the fans... they've been with me for a long time and were probably frustrated alongside me not getting there so I'm just delighted. Bobby Tambling is a great man, I was pleased to level it but I didn't want to overcook the celebration out of respect for him."

# ANSWERS

## PAGE 12-13 QUIZ PART 1

1. Wayne Rooney  2. Peter Crouch
3. Colombian  4. Ali Al-Habsi
5. Blackburn Rovers  6. Valencia
7. Sweden  8. Jussi Jaaskelainen
9. Thierry Henry
10. Marouane Fellaini (£15m)
11. Jonathan Walters  12. John Ruddy
13. Jonas Guttierez
14. James McClean
15. Benoit Assou-Ekotto
16. Juan Mata  17. Nathaniel Clyne
18. Adam Le Fondre
19. Chris Samba (£12m)  20. Michu

## PAGE 14-15 SPOT THE BOSS

## PAGE 22-23 QUIZ PART 2

21. Man United  22. Nottingham Forest
23. Notts County  24. Exeter City  25. Chelsea
26. Liverpool  27. Arsenal  28. Southampton

29. Stoke City  30. Man City  31. Chelsea
32. Millwall  33. West Brom
34. Norwich and Ipswich  35. Accrington Stanley
36. Stevenage  37. Aston Villa  38. Tottenham
39. Sunderland  40. Swansea City

## PAGE 28 TRANSFER TRAIL

**WAYNE ROONEY, Man United**
Bought from: Everton, International: England
**STEVEN FLETCHER, Sunderland**
Bought from: Wolves, International: Scotland
**YOHAN CABAYE, Newcastle**
Bought from: Lille, International: France
**MOUSSA DEMBELE, Tottenham**
Bought from: Fulham, International: Belgium
**SANTI CAZORLA, Arsenal**
Bought from: Malaga, International: Spain
**RAMIRES, Chelsea**
Bought from: Benfica, International: Brazil

**YOU WENT A FEW GAMES WITHOUT A GOAL BEFORE YOU HIT THAT RECORD. DID YOU THINK IT WAS STILL ON?**

"If I train hard and play regularly I think the goals will come. As a midfielder they can't come every game and you will go games without goals. If I keep my head up and play well the goals do come."

**A NUMBER OF SNIPERS SUGGESTED THAT MAYBE YOU WERE GETTING A BIT TOO OLD...**

"People look differently at you when you are the wrong side of 30 but I want to keep myself as fit as possible, to live right and keep my edge so I can keep competing at the top. I feel I've got a few more years in terms of top-class football and in an ideal world I would finish here but I wouldn't want to be here without performing."

**SO HOW LONG DO YOU THINK YOU CAN CARRY ON PLAYING AT THE TOP LEVEL?**

"Turning 35, I'd love to carry on as long as I can, and I feel I'm fit. I try to look after myself. I look at Ryan Giggs and he's as fit as a fiddle. He's the mark. I remember my ears pricking up when I heard about him doing yoga. I had to fight myself to do it as I like training outside, shooting and sprinting."

**MOURINHO?**

"The greatest manager in Chelsea's history. He changed the mentality of the place; gives us an edge and turns us into a consistent force."

SERGIO AGUERO, Man City
Bought from: Atletico Madrid, International: Argentina
JOE ALLEN, Liverpool
Bought from: Swansea, International: Wales

## PAGE 29 NAME THE PLAYERS

A. Jermain Defoe    B. John Terry
C. Hugo Loris    D. Tom Cleverley

## PAGE 34-35 QUIZ PART 3

41. Swansea 5 Bradford 0    42. Pavel Pogrebnyak
43. Moussa Sissoko    44. Ryan Giggs
45. Roman Abramovich    46. Oldham    47. True
48. The Pirates    49. Middlesbrough
50. Harry Redknapp    51. Alan Shearer
52. Man United    53. Steve Bruce    54. American
55. West Ham    56. Cardiff City    57. Uruguayan
58. Five goals in a Premier League game
59. Rangers 60. Fabio Capello

## PAGE 37 AROUND THE WORLD

A DC United, Washington, USA
B Flamengo, Rio de Janiero, BRAZIL
C Celtic, Glasgow, SCOTLAND
D Napoli, ITALY
E Shakhtar Donetsk, UKRANE
F Borrusia Dortmund, Dortmund, GERMANY
G CSKA Moscow, RUSSIA
H Benfica, Lisbon, PORTUGAL
I Panathinaikos, Athens. GREECE

## PAGE 38-39 WHICH BALL

GAME ONE E    GAME TWO C
GAME THREE E    GAME FOUR A

## PAGE 44 TRUE OR FALSE?

1. True  2. True  3. True  4. True  5. True  6. True  7. False  8. False  9. True  10. True

## PAGE 45 WAVE THE FLAG!

Geoff Cameron USA
Karim Benzema France
Steven Naismith Scotland
Marco Reus Germany
Demba Ba Senagal
Anders Lindegaard Denmark
Jonas Olsson Sweden
Jan Vertongham Belgium

## PAGE 50 WHERE AM I!

Peter Crouch Southampton, Stoke
Andy Carroll Newcastle, West Ham
Kevin Phillips West Brom, Crystal Palace
Jack Wilshere Bolton, Arsenal
David Bentley Birmingham, Blackburn
Tom Cleverley Watford, Man United
Yossi Benayoun Liverpool, Chelsea
Jermaine Jenas Tottenham, QPR

## PAGE 70-71 SPOT THE DIFFERENCE

## PAGE 74 GROUND GAME

Anfield, Liverpool, 45,000
City Ground, Nottingham Forest, 30,500
Amex Stadium, Brighton, 27,500
Emirates Stadium, Arsenal, 60,300
St James' Park, Newcastle United, 52,300
Old Trafford, Manchester United, 75,800

## PAGE 75 UNITED NATIONS

Goalkeeper: Jussi Jaaskelainen, Finland
Right back: Cesar Azpilicueta, Spain
Central defender: Vincent Kompany, Belgium
Central defender: Phil Jagielka, England
Left back: Davide Santon, Italy
Right wing: Antonio Valencia, Ecuador
Central midfielder: Yohan Cabaye, France
Central midfielder: Youssouf Mulumbu, DR Congo
Left wing: Gareth Bale, Wales
Striker: Dimitar Berbatov, Bulgaria
Striker: Demba Ba, Senegal

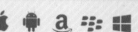